Breaking
Bad Habits

Breaking
Bad Habits

Defy Industry Norms and
Reinvigorate Your Business

Freek Vermeulen

Harvard Business Review Press

Boston, Massachusetts

Library of Congress Cataloging-in-Publication Data
Names: Vermeulen, Freek, author.
Title: Breaking bad habits : how to reinvigorate your business by defying industry norms / by Freek Vermeulen.
Description: Boston, Massachusetts : Harvard Business Review Press, [2017]
Identifiers: LCCN 2017019071 | ISBN 9781633693821 (hardcover : alk. paper)
Subjects: LCSH: Methods engineering. | Organizational change. | Experiential learning. | Creative ability in business. | Industrial management.
Classification: LCC T60.6 .V47 2017 | DDC 658.4/063—dc23 LC record available at https://lccn.loc.gov/2017019071

ISBN: 978-1-63369-382-1
eISBN: 978-1-63369-383-8

The paper used in this publication meets the requirements of the American National Standard for Permanence of Paper for Publications and Documents in Libraries and Archives Z39.48-1992.

CONTENTS

PART THREE

Reinvigorating Your Organization

PREFACE

Organizations are great; I love them. Not just because I make a living studying them, but because they are the true building blocks of human life. Organizations have produced or affected pretty much everything we touch, eat, wear, and see. They achieve and construct things that no individual could make, or sometimes even imagine.

However, organizations are also filled with practices—habitual ways of doing things—that are sometimes inefficient and bureaucratic, and that make our blood boil.

Sometimes these inefficient practices and strategies spread and persist for decades, or even longer. They persist just like viruses persist in nature. They take on lives of their own and continue operating despite leading to suboptimal results in the companies that embody them. The good news is that smart managers can purposefully identify and eradicate them, and then turn them into a profitable source of renewal and innovation. That is what this book is about.

Fertile Ground

Some years ago in London, I met a doctor who worked at an in vitro fertilization (IVF) clinic. After telling me about his field and the shape of the industry in the United Kingdom, he immediately—and vigorously—started discussing what he and others in the industry referred to as the "League Table," a government-mandated and publically accessible website with information on all the IVF clinics in the UK that the Human Fertilisation and Embryology Authority compiles and publishes annually. Since the website included information on each clinic's success rate, people had started treating it as a ranking.

The website was an admirable attempt to increase transparency and influence consumer behavior. Since most clinics in the UK are private (although there are a fair number of National Health Service clinics, too) and the procedure is expensive, the idea was to empower patients to go online, study the information, and make better choices about their medical care.

Even better, the reported success rates were based on objective data. In many businesses, you can debate whether something is a "success" or a "partial failure" and so on, but not in IVF. The percentage of births that result from treatment is clear-cut: either patients get pregnant or they don't.

Therefore, the League Table was intended to be good for both patients and clinics; the best clinics were rewarded for their high success rates and patients were empowered to seek out the best practitioners. But there was a problem that well-intentioned politicians had overlooked.

A clinic's *success rate* is not only driven by how skilled it is at performing the IVF procedure, but is also affected by the *quality of the input*, or the women who walk through the doors. Physiologically, some women are more receptive to IVF treatment than others, so a clinic's success rate is heavily weighted by the age, health, and fertility of the women it accepts as patients. For example, a clinic that only accepts women who are in their early twenties and are fertile, have never before undergone in vitro treatments, and have ample eggs that can be "freshly harvested" (as they say in the industry) would have high success rates. Whereas a clinic that also treats women in their forties who have unsuccessfully tried in vitro treatments in the past and only have a handful of eggs left over in the freezer from previous treatments would probably have lower success rates.

This was a problem. Since the success rates were measured and publicized so widely, and were known to influence consumer behavior, some clinics began to change their selection criteria to maximize their rankings. They practiced what I call *selection at the gate**: they purposely gravitated toward easier and more probable cases while avoiding more complicated ones. And this became a best practice in the industry.

Despite the short-term boost, selection at the gate wasn't good for anyone involved. Doctors and clinic administrators felt as if they were stuck between economics and education. As one doctor told me, "If your motivation for doing the job is to help patients or to expand your horizon scientifically, then, actually, you will choose to work

*After the Dutch expression *selectie aan de poort*.

in a clinic that is very diverse; you may particularly go out there and look for the difficult patients, because you can learn a lot from that." But if you choose to go that route, he continued, "you may well find yourself at a commercial disadvantage." Patients were disadvantaged as well, especially those who were considered difficult cases. A woman in her late thirties, for example, may have looked at the rankings and chosen a clinic with a high success rate, not knowing that that clinic wouldn't be interested in taking her on as a patient. Worse, she may have avoided a clinic with a low success rate, even though that clinic may have specialized in difficult cases such as hers.

This is just one textbook example of good intentions gone bad. The government was keen to measure IVF clinics, but these measures were imperfect representations of a clinic's success and what consumers really wanted to know. And, as is often the case, once officials began measuring things, clinics began optimizing for the measures (success rates), rather than the real thing (performance with all cases).

Unsurprisingly, this system had harmful effects on patients and the clinics that didn't practice selection at the gate. But the biggest victim may come as a surprise.

As my colleague Mihaela Stan and I discovered while researching the IVF industry, the practice probably did the most harm to the clinics that accepted *easy cases*. You read that right. After an initial surge of success, the clinics that tried to game the system ended up performing worse in the long run than their ethos-driven competitors.

Why? The learning curve.

Learning by Doing

The learning curve is a well-known phenomenon in management research; it shows that organizations pretty much automatically get better at what they produce. For example, as Boeing built more and more 737s, the process became easier and less expensive as time went on. Researchers have conducted such learning curve studies in many industries; I have seen studies on airplanes, cars, bottles, pizzas, and so on. And, as Stan and I discovered, the learning curve applied to IVF clinics as well.[1]

Figure I-1 displays the learning curves of the clinics that treated mostly good prognosis patients (labeled "high selection at the gate") and of the clinics that also admitted a

FIGURE I-1

The effects of selecting at the gate

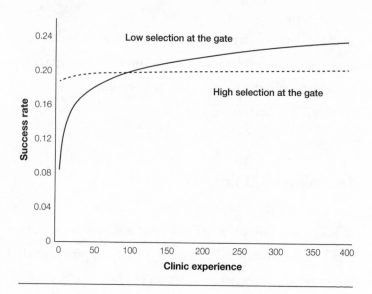

lot of poor prognosis patients ("low selection at the gate"). The vertical axis is the success rate, and the horizontal axis displays the clinic's experience.

As you can see, on the left side of the figure, as discussed, the clinics that admitted poor prognosis patients did much worse in terms of their success rate than the clinics that mostly treated easy cases, at first.

But you'll notice that selection at the gate had another effect that clinics hadn't anticipated: the success rate of those clinics increased a bit with experience, but not a whole lot—as shown by the almost horizontal line of the graph.

The clinics that treated a lot of poor prognosis patients, on the other hand, witnessed a sharp rise in their success rate; their learning curve is steep. It is so steep that after a year or so, the lines cross, and the clinics that treated quite a lot of poor prognosis patients actually started to display higher success rates than the clinics that thought they were being clever by treating good prognosis patients only. The clinics that did admit poor prognosis patients ended up doing significantly better in terms of their success rates, in spite of performing the procedure on a lot of poor prognosis patients.

Clearly, in the end, the good guys won.

Clinics learn a lot from poor prognosis cases. Figuring out how to help women who have a complicated etiology get pregnant leads to deeper knowledge, better communication patterns between specialists, and new, innovative procedures. Because of that, doctors were also able to use their new insights to improve standard cases as well.

The rankings-driven clinics aren't an anomaly. Organizations in every industry are harming themselves because of the best practices they've adopted and continue to use.

The good news, as I'll explore throughout this book, is that it's possible to identify these practices and kill them. By doing so, you can reduce harm, learn more, and eliminate inefficiencies. And, more important, by killing a bad practice, and not blindly following what your competitors are doing, you can gain a competitive edge and create a profitable source of renewal and innovation.

I'll explain all of that in more detail as we progress through the book. But, first, let's explore how bad practices are created, why they persist, and how they are negatively affecting your business in subtle but pernicious ways.

Best Bad Practices

Every organization follows a series of best practices: formal or informal rules of behavior that its employees have learned and passed along through the years. These include formalized management techniques, such as ISO 9000, total quality management, and Six Sigma; traits of organizational culture, such as the practice of working long hours in many corporate finance divisions in the banking industry; and various types of strategic choices, including which activities are performed and which are not.

In some cases, best practices live up to their name. They make our organizations faster, more efficient, and more competitive. For instance, the use of key performance indicators—in which a company systematically collects, analyzes, and communicates a set of performance metrics— helps firms to improve their productivity. Making promotion decisions based on merit surely is a helpful practice and beats simple tenure-based promotions. Similarly, conducting a cultural assessment increases the odds of successfully integrating an acquisition. Few would disagree that these represent good management practices.

But this isn't always the case. Some best practices are, in fact, inefficient; some are stupid; and some are plain harmful. Medical staff and administrators chase success rates. Financial and consulting firms still demand long hours from their employees, even when their demands lead to reduced productivity owing to overstress and burnout. And many pharmaceutical firms still spend billions on direct sales promotions for their blockbuster drugs in spite of the practice's proven ineffectiveness.[2] These so-called best practices, and countless others, prevent our organizations from creating new sources of innovation.

Examples of suspected bad practices are easy to find. All you need do is look around in your own organization.

Maybe it's the way your HR department handles performance reviews or how budgets are allocated. Or maybe it's your bonus system, the way your company assesses project proposals, or some other process that is too cumbersome or outdated.

With rare exceptions, managers do not willingly design and adopt harmful practices. Sure, sometimes self-interested managers do bad things, but I would argue that it's much more commonplace for good managers to inadvertently create something bad. Which, if you think about it, is more worrisome. It would be easier to dismiss the leadership of the IVF clinics that adopted the practice of selection at the gate as stupid or evil. But that wasn't the case. They genuinely thought that what they were doing made commercial sense. And it did . . . at first.

And because of the short-term benefits, which appeared quickly and were easy to see, the practice of selection at the gate spread. Once one clinic started the practice, and it became associated with success, others followed suit. And because they didn't foresee the long-term consequences, they continued with the practice.

The first reason that organizations follow bad practices is that we tend to believe in a Darwinian view of management. We believe that competition weeds out bad practices and props up the best ones. Therefore, we believe that the most successful firms must be following the best management practices, while unsuccessful firms are not. And, since those best practices help firms perform better, those are the ones that thrive and survive and gradually take over.

This isn't always true. Great companies aren't infallible; they make mistakes, too, and their processes and strategies can be just as inefficient and harmful as others'.

Second, organizations adopt bad practices because it enhances their legitimacy, as economic sociologists call it: companies are obliged to adopt or continue to follow a best practice because it is an industry norm, and if they choose not to follow it, investors, customers, and competitors will frown upon it.

For example, despite a retail chain's reservations about cultural differences, local competition, and supplier issues, it may feel pressure to enter the Chinese market because all of its competitors have done so and it seems like the legitimate thing to do. This is the same reason why a champagne maker may locate its operations in one of the traditional villages of Champagne rather than near Paris. Or why a management consulting firm chooses to adopt a traditional partnership structure instead of a more progressive model. Even though these options may be less economically feasible, they feel beholden to tradition. It's good optics. But it's not necessarily good business.

The third reason is as simple as it is frustrating. Sometimes we carry on with bad practices because that's the way it's always been done in our organizations. We side with the past and don't think twice about it. Most of the time, these practices don't start off as bad, but over time, as the organization or its competitive landscape changes, the practice becomes unsuitable. But no one questions it because we see its longevity as a sure sign of its continuing success.

Bad practices wouldn't be as much of a problem if our organizations were quick to change and adapt. But they aren't. Once adopted, a bad practice is hard to identify and often refuses to quit. And, like a virus, it begins to spread to other organizations.

How does this happen?

An Unholy Trinity

Three key conditions, in combination, make a detrimental management practice persist:

1. The practice is associated with success (as we briefly touched on above).

2. There is causal ambiguity in the industry.

3. The practice spreads more quickly than it kills.

Let's look at each of these conditions while returning to IVF clinics.

Condition 1: Association with Success

In order for a bad practice to take hold and become popular, it has to be associated with success in some way. This usually happens when an organization sees short-term results after its implementation, something we saw with IVF clinics.

Many firms in the IVF industry firmly and persistently believed that selection at the gate was a smart thing to do because it did lead to an increase in a clinic's success rate. So why mess with a good thing? Moreover, more clinics began adopting the process when they saw a competitor's success rate go up. They were convinced that it was a helpful practice. Hence, short-term success—even if outweighed by harmful long-term consequences—is one way that a bad practice becomes associated with an (erroneous) perception of success.

There are various ways that a harmful practice can become associated with success, and boosting short-term performance is only one of them. In the next chapter, we'll dive into the rest.

Condition 2: Causal Ambiguity

The second condition that needs to be in place for a bad or suboptimal practice to persist is causal ambiguity. In other words, people in the industry must not fully understand the practice's true long-term consequences.

This situation is what we witness in IVF, too. Whether a clinic is in trouble may be completely unambiguous; whether its success rate is lagging and the clinic is not innovative enough are usually quite evident to the organization's leadership. What is ambiguous is the connection between cause and effect—that the practice of selection at the gate (the cause) is hurting the organization's long-term success rate (its effect). That is because IVF is not a simple process; even for standard cases, seven of ten treatments fail. It's also because the harmful effects—a lack of opportunities for learning and innovation in the clinic—are soft and fluffy things, not hard factors that can be put into a spreadsheet and analyzed by hitting "Enter." Soft and fluffy things (innovation, learning, people) are often poorly understood in terms of their management but are very consequential for organizations' long-term success. A harmful practice feeds on causal ambiguity; it needs it to survive.

Condition 3: Spreads Quicker Than It Kills

The third condition for a harmful practice to thrive is that it needs to be simple—simple enough to be adopted easily by organizations in the industry, incumbents and entrants alike. Take note: a harmful practice is hardly ever a complex practice. Complex practices spread only with difficulty, and just as a virus must hop quite swiftly from one person to the next to survive, a bad management practice must hop easily from one firm to another.

In the IVF industry, selection at the gate is easy to adopt; it merely involves observing some simple patient demographics (e.g., age), background information (e.g., whether the patient has often failed treatment before), and a battery of standard tests (e.g., on ovarian reserve). Consequently, other clinics imitate it easily and the bad practice reproduces.

Introduction

Swift diffusion is fostered by other factors, too, including industry characteristics, such as a homogeneous and dense population of firms (as in the IVF industry), but it is insufficient by itself; the rate of diffusion also needs to be high relative to the rate at which the practice deteriorates adopting firms. Think about it: a virus can only survive if it spreads quicker than it kills its host, that is, if it hops onto other people before the original host succumbs. That's true for organizations, too. Just as a highly lethal virus that kills almost instantaneously cannot survive because it will die with its host before it has been able to infect anyone else, harmful practices are also never highly toxic. If a practice were to put a firm at a huge competitive disadvantage from its onset, it would swiftly die out with that firm. Harmful practices are much sneakier: they weaken a firm just a little bit, wearing it out gradually over the long run.

Each one of these three conditions needs to be present for bad practices to be able to exist. When they occur in combination, the effects are truly troublesome, making a harmful practice persist, roving further afield and weakening its hosts.

Yet, these conditions are quite common. Practices often have different consequences in the long run than in the short run, and there are many other reasons why a practice can be erroneously associated with success. Causal ambiguity is commonplace in most industries where change is almost constant and many factors can influence firm performance. Similarly, exchanges of personnel, imitation of each others' practices and decisions through benchmarking exercises, and the use of consultants and other advisers—all of which stimulate the diffusion of a practice—are the norm in most businesses rather than the exception. Thus, bad practices are prevalent and prevail.

Here Lies the Opportunity

Before we move forward into part one of the book, I want to reiterate an important point. Yes, some best practices are harmful and inefficient, as I'll continue to describe in detail, and, yes, killing them will eliminate their harmful effects and inefficiencies. But the main point I want to get across is that killing bad practices can open up new avenues for growth and innovation and reinvigorate your business. That's really what this book is about.

Low-cost airlines such as Southwest, for example, have attracted new consumers, many of whom would have traveled by car, train, or bus, by eliminating in-flight meals and other amenities that traditional airlines were convinced people wanted. By eliminating these bad practices, Southwest and others were able to lure new customers to their airlines with lower prices.

In part two and throughout the book, I'll touch on other examples, including how the *Independent* increased its circulation by printing its newspaper on smaller pages. We'll also explore how businesses have made killing best practices the central part of their business model. The founders of citizenM avoided most of the trappings of mid-range hotels, and Eden McCallum, a management consulting firm, was able to attract top talent by hiring all of its consultants on a per-project, freelance basis.

In part three, I'll lay out a more long-term strategy for building organizations that seek to change and renew themselves continually, which will drastically reduce the possibilities of bad practices emerging and doing further harm to businesses.

But, first, in part one, I want to circle back to the origins of bad management practices and dive deeper into the three conditions that enable them to breed and persist.

How Bad Practices Prevail

CHAPTER 1

We're Suckers for Success

At the end of World War II, in 1945, the Japanese economy was devastated. Industrial areas were destroyed in almost all major cities, transportation networks were severely damaged, a quarter of Japan's national wealth was annihilated, and more than two million people in its workforce were killed. The country's population suffered for a decade.

Yet, by the 1960s, Japan's economy started growing rapidly and unabatedly. In what became known as Japan's "economic miracle," it quickly rose to become the second-largest economy in the world. Where, in 1965, Japan's gross domestic product stood at about $90 billion, by 1980, it had increased to over $1 trillion. Much of this was achieved through exports. Japanese car manufacturers, for example, were outcompeting the traditional Western brands in their home markets. Japanese cars—such as Toyota, Honda, and Mitsubishi—were more affordable but also of significantly higher quality. American car manufacturers, among others, were eager to learn how the Japanese companies managed to achieve this.

A large part of their success could be ascribed to a set of new management practices referred to as total quality management (TQM).

In the 1950s, Americans W. Edwards Deming and Joseph Juran had gone to Japan to lecture on quality management, and their views concurred with those of local management professor Kaoru Ishikawa. TQM—as the practices they advocated became widely known—prescribed how all aspects of an organization should be committed to delivering quality: not only top to bottom within the organization, but also start to finish in the entire product life cycle (see the sidebar "The Core Components of TQM").

The Core Components of TQM

Worker involvement

Whereas, in most companies, management and engineers organized and controlled the production process, while line employees were merely expected to execute their prescribed tasks, TQM advocated much greater involvement of ordinary workers in the organization of the process.

Top management's responsibility

Senior management's foremost task was to create an environment in which workers would feel safe and able to contribute and improve the functioning of the organization. Managers should remove

(*continued*)

Overall, TQM required a long-term, cooperative, and comprehensive approach to doing business. In order to be successful, organizations needed to continuously improve their processes and deliver high-quality products and services that were useful to customers. By doing so, they would grow and gain market share while uniting all organizational systems that create fear, such as punishment for poor performance or appraisal systems that explicitly ranked employees.

Intrinsic motivation

TQM assumed that employees have an intrinsic motivation to perform their tasks well, that they enjoy the feeling of accomplishment, and that they are motivated to contribute to the prosperity of the organization. The assumption resulted, for instance, in relying on self-managed work teams as a form of empowerment.

Cross-functional solutions

Since organizations are systems of interdependent parts, TQM advocated for ad hoc cross-functional

employees around a common goal and providing them with job satisfaction and security. From all this, profits would follow.

And, indeed, Japan's multinationals kept growing and flourishing with TQM.

teams that could identify and solve quality problems. Other permanent cross-functional teams were then responsible for the improvement of processes over the long term.

Evidence-driven decisions

Front-line employees are the ones who should analyze and control processes. TQM also advocated for the use of systematic data collection, statistics, and testing solutions by experiment to solve problems and generate process improvements, rather than relying on impressions and conjectures.

Continuous improvement

On top of that, organizations should constantly collect and analyze data in order to improve the

(continued)

So it's no surprise that American companies, many of which were watching their market share dwindle, were eager to replicate Japanese companies that adopted TQM and, with it, their successes. Consulting companies also jumped onto the bandwagon and began offering TQM accuracy of conclusions, aid consensus and decision making, and allow for predictions based on past data. In the TQM view, quality improvement should be treated as a never-ending quest, involving all employees in the organization.

Customer and supplier relationships

Finally, creating quality was thought to transcend the boundaries of the organization, and should be determined by the requirements of customers. Moreover, companies should establish long-term supplier partnerships rather than engage in ad hoc transactions. Thus, TQM was a comprehensive management approach that involved all stakeholders in an organization.

workshops and implementation programs. If it worked in Japan, why not in the United States?

TQM became all the rage in the 1980s and early 1990s, but there was one problem: the American companies that adopted it didn't find nearly the same successes as their Japanese counterparts.

Imperfect Copies

Western companies ran into trouble because they created imperfect copies of TQM. They often only adopted its most visible, tangible elements or they set up cross-functional teams and gave people access to data about quality levels, but failed to create the organizational climate needed for employees to feel secure enough to suggest and implement improvements. They abolished end controls without having nurtured a sense of responsibility for errors throughout the organization. Top managers also thought they could outsource TQM's implementation to consultants, without realizing their close involvement was necessary to signal quality management as the key focus of the entire organization. Thus, since the resulting TQM copy was imperfect, lacking the nuances and complexities of its original, it became useless at best and harmful at worst.

Replicating a successful management practice is a very difficult task. As professors Sidney Winter from the Wharton School and Gabriel Szulanski from INSEAD argued, organizational practices—especially those that lead to competitive advantage—are often highly complex.[1] They consist of multiple components, some of them tangible (such as technologies and procedures), but many of them tacit and intangible (such as organizational culture and informal networks), that are subtlety interwoven. These practices, which developed and evolved over many years, are often so complex that the firms that implemented them aren't completely sure how they work. So it's no surprise that Western firms erred. They took a highly complex system and reduced it to something much simpler.

They also added new features to the system, some of which ran counter to the spirit of TQM. As professors J. Richard Hackman from Harvard University and Ruth Wageman from Columbia University discovered, a majority of American organizations added performance measurement and financial reward systems that rewarded employees for achieving quality goals.[2] Although rewards and incentives are commonplace in many organizations, they were antithetical to the philosophy of TQM, and Deming himself explicitly argued that they were counterproductive.

This is a very common pattern. In an attempt to replicate a best practice, firms end up transforming a complex practice into a much simpler one, and this simplified version, which is much more alluring and easier to copy, is transferred from one firm to the next, becoming less and less useful—and eventually harmful.

Yet, the American managers weren't deliberately adopting a deleterious practice; they were genuinely trying to improve their organizations. They did what managers often do: they looked around them to see what seemed to work for others. And TQM was a great success in Japan, so it seemed to make sense to try to emulate it.

But, in the end, they, like all of us, became suckers for success. They blindly adopted a practice based on nothing but its prior success, implemented it poorly, and then overlooked its nefarious effects once they committed to it.

Unfortunately, poor replication is only one of many ways a practice's association with success can lead organizations astray. Let's look at a few others.

Benchmarking Is BS

Managers often unknowingly adopt bad practices when they try to benchmark their organizations against the other companies in their industries.

I see this all the time in my own home organization, London Business School. Whenever, for instance, an MBA curriculum review is being discussed, some dean or senior administrator will say, "Let's do some benchmarking." Which means: "Let's see what others are doing (and then do it too)." The outcome of such a benchmarking exercise is usually a list of ten or so of our main competitor business schools (i.e., Harvard, INSEAD, Wharton, and so on), of which, say, seven have adopted a particular course structure. Then, some top dog says, "So, we should really do it too," and everybody nods. This is a wonderful way for a bad practice to spread.

Not everyone needs to be doing something for us to believe it's a good thing. Sometimes just the top performers need to be doing it. This is because we are all inclined to pay the most attention to the best-performing companies in our industry and only to those. For instance, some years ago, whenever GE did something new (such as Six Sigma), many firms were inclined to immediately imitate it. Like a lot of people, the managers at these organizations assumed that GE's leaders knew it all: "Surely, when they do it, it must be a good thing, because they're such a successful firm."

Indeed, research has confirmed that organizations tend to imitate the actions of other companies that stand out as successful, even when it is clear that the newly developed practice is not the cause of the company's success.[3]

The press does it, too. Journalists habitually write about top-performing companies and interview their CEOs, rather than the average Joes. We, admittedly, do it in business schools: we teach cases about the best, blue-chip companies, ignoring the less-sexy average types.

Blame It on Perception Bias

In an experiment I performed at the London Business School with my former PhD student Xu Li (now an assistant professor at the European School of Management and Technology in Berlin), we noticed that focusing on the "best" is a very general and human trait.

Li and I asked people to look at a file that contained information about a thousand firms, including ten years of performance data on each and how they ranked over the course of the ten years. Firms could follow one of three strategies, which we generically labeled A, B, or C (in order not to bias people in any way toward one or the other). We displayed this information on a computer screen so that we could unobtrusively use eye-tracker technology to monitor what they were paying attention to. We then asked participants a simple question: which strategy do you think leads to the highest performance, on average?

Monitoring their eye movements, we noticed that people usually first started scanning the entire content of the file; they looked at individual firms in detail, their financial performance, and the strategies they followed. However, after a short while—usually no more than a couple of minutes—they gave up trying to assess every individual company: there were just too many. Then they turned to a simple course of action: they glanced over the file, looking for one particular thing among the different firms: their performance rank among the thousand companies. As soon as they spotted a high-ranking firm, their eyes stopped scanning, and they assessed the firm in more detail, specifically focusing on what strategy (A, B, or C) the particular company was following. Toward the end of the file, they had seen enough and had made up their minds; a large majority of people concluded that strategy B was the superior strategy.

However, they were wrong: strategy B, on average, led to significantly lower financial performance.

How come the majority of people got it so wrong in this experiment? Because of one simple manipulation that we did, but one that occurs all the time in reality: the different strategies (A, B, and C) also led to different levels of variance in firm performance.

The performance of the firms following strategy A or C was quite evenly distributed: most firms performed pretty well, although there were also some that slightly underperformed and a handful that performed really well.

The performance of firms following strategy B, by contrast, was much more varied. Most of them underperformed, with some doing really quite poorly, but a good number performed really, really well: they were among the top performers in the industry.

How come then that people got it wrong, thinking that strategy B on average led to the best performance (while it led to the worst)? That's because they were drawn to the top performers. Since most of the very top-performing companies had adopted B, the participants concluded that B must have been the best strategy for everyone. But they were wrong. These firms were merely the exceptions to the rule. (See figure 1-1.)

We experienced real-world confirmation of this bias when we interviewed members of the Chinese pharmaceutical industry who told us that companies that engaged in new product development had outperformed those who didn't from 1991 to 2000 (the first decade of privatization in the industry). Yet, when we analyzed the real numbers, clearly the opposite was true. But, as with the firms that

FIGURE 1-1

Variance-induced perception bias

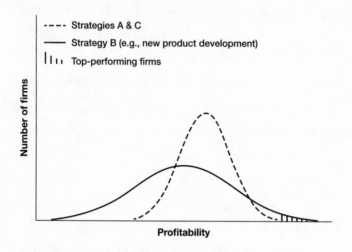

Strategy A and Strategy C had identical results, so only one curve is shown here.

adopted strategy B in our experiment, their variance was much higher—so much higher that, indeed, the few top performers were often new product developers. When we asked the interviewees to justify their answers, they cited the top-performing companies in their industry as a case in point.

Like the participants in our experiment, the interviewees overlooked the fact that most firms that adopted a new product development strategy performed below the industry average. They—like all of us—focused solely on the few best-performing ones.

Champions Are Deceptive

Practices don't spread by themselves; when a firm is contemplating adopting a particular new practice, the practice will often have an internal champion, someone who is convinced that it's a good idea. And the champion will try to convince others in the firm of its merits.

To promote the practice, the champion will often invite a speaker or two from other firms that have experience with it. Needless to say, he or she won't invite someone from a firm in which the practice was a complete and outright failure; no, the champion will make sure the invited speakers are equally committed to and enthusiastic advocates of the practice. As professor Mark Zbaracki discovered in his famous study, this is one of the reasons why TQM spread so rapidly: external speakers exaggerated its benefits and glossed over the occasions when it did not work.[4]

Subsequently, firms will begin to test the waters by implementing the practice in a few units. After a trial period, the internal champion will invite representatives from some of these units to talk about their experiences to units that haven't adopted the practice. These internal champions—as was the case with the spread of TQM—act in similar ways as the guest speakers, and so they help to proliferate the myth.

Because these information sessions endow the practice with success from the very start, the harmful practice spreads quickly and is difficult to kill. Since the practice has worked wonders in other organizations, no one questions its success. If there's a problem, managers blame the implementation, not the practice itself. So the practice remains associated with success—and survives.

Quick Wins Make Us Losers

Once a practice is adopted and brings on immediate results, its association with success grows. We've seen this already with IVF clinics: genuine short-term benefits (higher rankings and prestige) can confer an association with success upon a particular practice or strategy. But, in the long run, the effects can be negative.

I'm often surprised that this surprises people. Everybody understands that short-term effects are often different from long-run consequences. That's the whole idea behind investing in something: we accept short-term pain (money out the door) in return for bigger, long-term gain (more money coming through the door). Often it works the other way around, too. A bit of short-term gain can cause a lot of long-term pain.

I strongly believe that whenever an organization is deciding whether to adopt a particular new practice, strategy, or process, it should first explicitly raise the question, "What might be the consequences in the long run?" Then it should think through the long-term consequences, because, of course, these might be different from the short-term ones.

Time Moves On, but Practices Linger

The last factor might also be the most important, because I suspect it's the most common: the transfer of a practice from a different context or time when it did bring benefits.

In this case, the practice did not start out as harmful, but as time passed or circumstances changed, it became inappropriate. But because of its initial association with success, it persists.

Many of the ways in which firms have organized themselves—their structures, their formal and informal processes and systems—are there for historical reasons: someone at some point decided a particular thing would work best, and the firm stuck with it for years, if not decades.

This is not necessarily bad if circumstances don't change, but business environments have the nasty habit of changing all the time. The best way of doing things then isn't necessarily the best way of doing things now. But often companies—and whole industries—are slow to adapt.

Consider, for example, buyback guarantees in book publishing. In the 1930s, during the Great Depression in the United States, many bookshops—largely small, independent stores—could no longer afford to buy books from publishers to sell in their stores. To keep sales going, Simon & Schuster began to guarantee booksellers that they could return any unsold books at the publisher's expense;

the store owners would only have to pay for the books they sold. The practice was a success because it enabled Simon & Schuster to continue selling books, even though its direct clients had little money. Soon other publishers followed suit, until everybody in the industry did it that way. The practice persists to this day. Or, as an executive of Beacon Press put it to me, "[The practice] seems to be a permanent feature of the American publishing and bookselling scene."

However, at present, when times have changed and booksellers are also organized in large chain stores and companies—such as Waterstones and Barnes & Noble—buyback guarantees lead to great, unnecessary inefficiencies.

Publishers must bear the risks and costs of printing, and the return logistics for and the pulping of unsold books. Booksellers have comparatively little incentive to accurately forecast sales, but because they initiate the numbers to order, the publishers are deprived of the necessary market information that would enable them to optimize their production planning. All this makes for a highly inefficient system. Yet, the practice of buyback guarantees persists, because that is how everybody is doing it and has always done it. The practice of buyback guarantees was useful at some point in time—a time long lost.

I have no doubt that every industry and every organization engages in practices that made sense at some point but which they have continued ever since, even though circumstances have changed. Transfer from a time long lost—when it was useful—is a prime way that a bad practice becomes cognitively associated with success, in spite of its being harmful in the present. But—as I discuss later—this situation can offer truly superb opportunities for innovation.

Bad Practices Persist

These are the prime reasons why harmful practices become associated with success—which explains why organizations may initially be inclined to adopt a practice in spite of its consequences. However, in terms of theorizing, reasons to adopt something do not necessarily equate to reasons to stick with it.

Hopefully you've become convinced that organizations sometimes get suckered into adopting bad practices. But why would they not simply discard them after some time, you might wonder? It doesn't make sense: why don't organizations learn—from observing their own fate or that of others—and simply abandon a bad practice after gaining some experience with it, and do something else, something that does make sense?

The short answer is, it's complicated. Bad practices persist in circumstances where they are difficult to spot, especially in real time. Which brings us to the next condition: causal ambiguity.

CHAPTER 2

Causal Ambiguity

My former colleague at London Business School, Markus Reitzig, was really into studying patents. Frankly, I didn't quite get his fascination with them, but one day he discovered something that I found quite intriguing. Together with his coauthor Stefan Wagner, he noticed that more and more firms chose to outsource a particular aspect of their patenting process: the filing and enforcement of patents.[1] As you probably know, firms that do R&D usually try to protect their inventions through patenting. Once a patent is granted, they often need to enforce it, sometimes through proactive and reactive litigation. These different types of activities—patent filing and patent enforcement— are so specialized that different departments within the organization usually carry them out.

Reitzig noticed that firms would increasingly outsource the patent filing to an external, specialized law firm in order to cut costs and improve efficiency. However, one of the crucial activities conducted for patent filing before the patent is applied for is the identification of "prior art," which encompasses any possible evidence available to the public that the invention might already be known. If a firm outsources the entire patent-filing activity, it also leaves this identification and interpretation of prior art to an outside party. That, as it turns out, has some unanticipated consequences; mainly, it prevents companies from gaining knowledge about technology competitors that may be infringing on their copyrights. Reitzig suspected that losing such knowledge could prove crucial further down the line.

Reitzig and Wagner began to examine 189,332 patent applications by 504 different firms. They studied those firms that had outsourced patent filing and statistically compared them with those that had continued to perform both activities in-house. They found that the firms that had handled the filings themselves were much better at identifying potential technology competitors—and their strengths and weaknesses—early on. This allowed these firms to successfully attack their competitors proactively. Firms that turned their own in-house patent-filing function over to some external specialist found themselves ill-equipped to enforce their patents. Consequently, their downstream performance plummeted. Hence, outsourcing one part of the value chain—and saving some costs in the process—unexpectedly led to substantial problems in a different part of the firm's value chain.

This wasn't what the outsourcing firms had bargained for.

The Fog of Cause and Effect

What Reitzig and Wagner found for patenting is true for many activities; a decision to simplify a process and lower costs can have undesirable consequences for some other function somewhere else within the firm. And since the causal links are largely unknown and often impossible to observe, quantify, and measure—and often take a while to materialize—firms don't learn from their mistakes.

More alarming, even when a firm notices that something is wrong, say, that it's underperforming in terms of patent enforcement, more often than not it still doesn't abandon the process. Why? The link between cause and effect is too ambiguous. The firms that outsource their patent filing, for example, can't see that the practice—which they may have implemented years ago—is making them so lousy at patent enforcement. There's too much ambiguity.

Causal ambiguity exists because the relationships between various parts of an organization are complex and multifaceted, meaning that many variables are influencing the outcome (e.g., patent enforcement performance) in various ways, with several of them operating with delays.

The other problem is that the long-term effects of a process are vague and abstract, whereas its short-term benefits are clear and immediate. For example, firms that outsourced parts of their patent processes couldn't quite comprehend how their decision limited their understanding of competitors and their innovation efforts and thus limited their readiness in responding to competitors' actions. The same goes for IVF clinics: in the short term, it wasn't clear that rejecting difficult cases was leading to communication lapses between the various specialists involved in the procedure; less in-depth, tacit knowledge of the conditions that necessitated the procedure; and a general deficit of innovation. Why? Because *learning* and *tacit knowledge* and *communication patterns* are fluffy, difficult-to-grasp concepts.

As a consequence, the bad practice remains in place.

A Vice Called ISO (or Any Process Management System)

When Mary Benner was a PhD student at Columbia Business School—later a professor at Wharton—she decided to study an organizational practice that she had experienced when working as a manager at Honeywell: ISO 9000, a so-called process management system. A process management system offers guidelines and techniques for companies to map and improve their internal processes and ensure that all units in their organization adhere to them. It focuses on reducing variation in how processes are conducted, while allowing for ongoing incremental improvements, in order to generate efficiency gains and improve customer satisfaction. Hence, like TQM and Six Sigma, ISO 9000 was developed to boost quality and efficiency by standardizing best practices in an organization.

In the 1990s, when Benner was at Honeywell, ISO 9000 was all the rage. Or, as Benner said, "For years, management consultants and many academics have told companies that they should 'document what they do and do what they document.' That is, they should pay close attention to tightly routinizing their processes to reduce costs and improve quality." ISO 9000, people said, really works, and indeed many companies experienced efficiency gains and reduced error rates. Consequently, there were plenty of eager adopters and dedicated consultants heralding its wonderful benefits.

Yet, Benner had grown quite skeptical of the likes of ISO 9000 and, together with her PhD adviser, Michael Tushman, decided to study them. In particular, she was interested in documenting the long-term impact of management systems, specifically their impact on a firm's innovation output. Her hypothesis was that, although management systems were useful in stable business environments, where efficiency and reliability are key, they could be harmful in more dynamic environments. She said, "If the environment is changing—for example, if the company's existing technology is headed for obsolescence because of the introduction of new technologies—then inwardly focused attention to process and its associated effects on innovation and change can impede an organization's ability to respond to changes in their working environment." To put it another way, you can't innovate by always doing the same thing in the same way.

Benner conducted a large-scale study of the impact of ISO 9000 in two very different industries: the paint industry (a relatively stable industry) and the photography industry (a turbulent, fast-changing business). She tracked all the innovations for 119 firms over a twenty-year period and noted when they adopted the ISO 9000 system. She found that in both industries, ISO 9000 was perfectly OK in terms of allowing for incremental innovation (i.e., variations on whatever the firm was already doing), but that it was a dud when it came to real innovation, the stuff that enables a firm to renew itself and adapt to a changing environment.[2] And adaptation is what keeps a firm alive.

But despite the drawbacks that Benner exposed, companies continue to use process management systems, such as ISO 9000, even in environments where innovation and swift adaptation are crucial. Till death do them part.

Here again, causal ambiguity is at the heart of the problem. People have trouble understanding the connection between the cause (implementing ISO 9000 or a similar management process) and its effect (reduced innovation).

One reason for this is that the effect usually occurs only several years down the line; implementing a process management system does not block innovation instantaneously. The time lag makes it harder to understand what is causing its reduction. By the time the evil properties take effect, the practice's initial implementation is all but a distant memory.

Moreover, innovation is a soft and fuzzy process. There are many factors that influence an organization's success in innovation—skill sets, culture, systems, and processes—and they're all connected. Which is why, again, most managers are blind to the fact that their adherence to a management system is what was slowing them down.

Even when the relationship between ISO 9000 and innovation is explained to people, they still have a hard time getting their head around it and accepting it for what it is. As Benner said, "The main obstacle has been getting people to be willing to question assumptions about the universal and unambiguous benefits of process management. I encountered a lot of resistance when I first presented the work several years ago."

I have experienced similar resistance whenever I've questioned process management systems in environments where innovation is important, for instance, in a class with executives, while explaining Benner's work. Often I've encountered several people who eagerly agreed (seemingly because they had been having suspicions about these systems all along), but usually a couple of participants could just not consider that ISO 9000 or Six Sigma—or whatever process management system they had been implementing during their careers—might have downsides in the long run.

The key thing to remember is that universal and unambiguous benefits—as Benner put it—are really just a pipe dream: too good to be true. Practices usually have good and bad consequences—as most things in life have—and considering only the good ones while denying the possible existence of bad ones is a recipe for disaster.

Bad Practices Are Clever

Complicating matters further, even if companies notice the harmful effects of their bad practices—a dearth of innovation, sluggish patent enforcement, or whatever it may be—they don't often notice or understand what is causing them. Thus, they not only adopt bad practices but also stick with them, even when their company's performance is taking a turn for the worse.

A hard-core capitalist might proclaim that that's the beauty of competition and that we don't need companies to understand the error of their ways, because competitive forces will just blindly drive out the weak ones, annihilating their crappy practices in the process. Unfortunately, that's not necessarily true; harmful practices can be cleverer than that, and we'll see that play out in a rather gruesome example from anthropology in the next chapter.

CHAPTER 3

They Spread Quicker Than They Kill

The Fore people are a large tribe of approximately twenty thousand in the Okapa district in a mountainous region of the Eastern Highlands of Papua New Guinea. In the nineteenth century, as in many societies and cultures, they buried the bodies of their dead. But, at some point—probably toward the end of that century—the Fore people began to consume their deceased relatives. Anthropologists refer to the practice as endocannibalism or mortuary cannibalism, which are just fancy words that mean: someone dies, then you eat them.

This new ritual emerged, as anthropologists put it, for "purely gastronomic reasons." Famine was a real problem among the Fore, so the practice had its advantages. Eating your deceased relative, rather than putting him or her in the ground, was a creative solution to food shortages.

As far as I know, no record exists of exactly where and when the practice began, but we do know that it began spreading, and fairly rapidly, throughout the southern villages. Before long, all the Fore people had adopted the new ritual. The practice's benefits were clear, universal, and unambiguous: the Fore were no longer hungry.

The practice, however, also caused a severe problem. Because the Fore people consumed every part of their deceased relatives, including the brain, they gradually began to develop a nerve disease, which they referred to as kuru. A progressive disease that caused severe physiological and neurological effects, kuru was deadly; it was a variant of Creutzfeldt-Jacob (or "mad cow") disease. Because of the practice's wide usage, the Fore people started dying by the dozens, the hundreds, and eventually the thousands.

Yet, the necro-gastronomic practice continued until approximately 1960, when Australian forces put an end to it (and not because the Australians understood that it led to the disease; they just thought it was gross). By then, about half the Fore had succumbed to kuru. They continued dying for another decade or so, given the disease's incubation period, but then kuru gradually declined and then vanished.[1]

How Bad Practices Persist

This practice of the Fore people obviously is an extreme example, but also an interesting one because it puzzled anthropologists. They did not understand—at least at first—why natural selection did not weed out this clearly detrimental ritual. It is interesting to me because business economics and management practices work in much the same way. Economists and managers assume that management practices that put firms at a competitive disadvantage will disappear. But reality shows that they don't.

Anthropologists had long assumed that cultural practices such as rituals and customs persist because they are useful and beneficial. They thought that harmful practices, on the other hand, would diminish via competition; the tribes that adopted them would grow weak as a result and gradually disappear, taking the practices with them. In this view, long-lasting rituals and practices must benefit a tribe in some way or another; otherwise, the practices would not have lasted. And even if a practice might seem silly or detrimental, if you dig deep enough—say, through an elaborate ethnographic study—you should be able to grasp its benefits.

Sometimes, such research indeed uncovers how a seemingly bad practice is in fact useful after all. For example, anthropologists first thought that the breastfeeding practices among the !Kung San bushmen, where women breastfed so long that it led to fewer children (because women generally are less fertile while breastfeeding), was counterproductive. But given that the women had to carry children while traveling long distances, the anthropologists determined that the practice was beneficial to the tribe because having fewer children increased their survival rates.

However, over time, it has become increasingly clear that there are also anomalies: rituals and customs that really were harmful and affected the life expectancy of the people practicing them, sometimes threatening the survival of whole tribes altogether. Let's face it: female circumcision is just plain stupid; there's no hidden benefit. Similarly, foot binding in

China—crippling women—was unambiguously detrimental. And the tattooing practices in Polynesia, which often proved fatal for the person receiving the tattoos, were also just plain daft. How come, then, these bad practices did not die out? Perhaps the people and tribes were not able to grasp their own daftness, but surely the practices would die with the demise of the tribes? But they did not; some of these detrimental practices persisted for centuries or longer. Some (unfortunately) persist at this writing.

Many economists, managers, and politicians share the same blind belief in natural selection, thinking it will automatically make bad practices disappear. But they are wrong. Bad practices spread and slowly hurt our organizations just as kuru harmed the Fore people. Let me explain how it works.

A Bad Practice as a Slow but Serial Killer

A harmful practice can only survive if it kills slowly. In addition, it must spread easily and rapidly. Just as the most lethal viruses never take off and persist, the most harmful cultural and management practices don't make it because they die out. If a virus nearly instantaneously kills its host, the virus will die with the demise of its victims, because it cannot live outside of a host (just as a practice cannot exist outside of an organization). Similarly, behavioral practices—whether cultural or organizational—will not survive if they kill their host quickly.

The Fore's gastronomic invention spread swiftly because it was easy to imitate. People in the next village could quite effortlessly switch from burials to this new culinary practice because all they had to do was observe it at their neighbors' and then they were ready to dig in too. Ease of diffusion is a necessity for a harmful practice to spread and persist.

Ease of diffusion can thus come from the practice itself: it has to be simple enough to be imitated swiftly. A harmful practice is seldom complex and difficult to learn; it's the simple practices you have to look out for. This means that organizations can easily imitate a simple practice from others, but it also means that new employees can simply adopt it from an organization's own past, and that new entrants adapt effortlessly to the norms in the industry and practice it too. Hence, the detrimental practice persists.

Sometimes bad practices get a bit of help. In IVF, for example, medical professionals all attend the same conferences and read the same periodicals as others in their specialty. And personnel often move between clinics. Just as viruses are helped by intense contact between people, bad practices thrive on it too. Moreover, bad practices often diffuse via third parties—usually consultants, or board members, or accountants. Various consulting agencies heavily promoted ISO 9000, for example, with a central organization overseeing its spread. Similarly, ample management consultants have preached and implemented outsourcing. That's how bad practices thrive: fast diffusion, slow death, and a little help from your friends.

The death is so slow—although likely agonizing—because of the practice's incubation time. While the organization is still healthy, and perhaps even outperforming its peers (in the short run), others will be tempted to imitate it. Selection in IVF does not immediately depress a clinic's success rate—quite the contrary—it may take several years until the deprivation of learning opportunities (from treating difficult cases) lowers the clinic's performance. Similarly, outsourcing and ISO 9000 may lead to trouble only in the long run.

Over time, others may imitate the practice and then the practice begins to spread before anyone realizes it's harmful. We're bad at spotting bad practices, even after they've spread and caused harm, because of our widespread belief in market efficiency.

The Unholy Trinity

Slow impairment, along with an association with success and casual ambiguity, forms an unholy trinity that allows bad practices to spread and persist despite their harmful effects.

Bad practices are covert killers. Since their effects are subtle and slow, you may not realize that a practice you implemented years ago is making your innovation pipeline run dry, your employees demotivated or unprepared, or your customers frustrated.

But that's why it's crucial to identify bad practices and eliminate them, something I'll cover next in part two. If you do so, you'll also discover new paths to growth and innovation while reinvigorating your business in the process.

Eliminating Bad Practices

CHAPTER 4

The Tale of the Giant Newspapers

For a long time, probably much longer than I'd like to admit, I was perplexed by the size of newspapers. I couldn't understand why they were printed in the broadsheet format, which made them big, flimsy, and difficult to read.

I'm not sure when my pet peeve originated, but my good friend Henk-Jan Bruil remembers us talking about it while we were both attending university in the town of Tilburg in the Netherlands. Back then, we used to sip coffee and talk in the basement of the school (he probably smoked a self-rolled cigarette or two as well), nursing hangovers after spending our evenings at Polly Maggoo or another bar in town. According to Bruil, one day, while we were killing time between classes, I began complaining about how flipping and folding newspaper pages made for a subpar reading experience in comparison to magazines.

My newspaper fixation dogged me for years. After I graduated and finished my PhD in business economics, I began consulting for the top management team at Perscombinatie Meulenhoff (PCM), the largest Dutch newspaper company at the time. PCM owned all the large Dutch newspapers except the *Telegraaf*, and all of these, like most of the other newspapers in the world, favored the broadsheet format. Because I had the ears of the executives, I asked why they didn't make their papers smaller. Since they were veterans of the newspaper trade, I was hoping that one of them would offer a clear-cut explanation. Instead, they looked at me quizzically and said, "Freek. Look around you. Every quality newspaper in the world is big; customers wouldn't want a smaller version."

For years, that conversation lingered in my mind. There had to be a reason for printing in a large format, I thought.

Eventually, I settled on the idea that printing the news on large pieces of paper was probably cheaper.

Sometime later, after I became an assistant professor of strategic and international management at London Business School, I did some advisory work for several executives of the very English, left-ish newspaper the *Guardian* and its Sunday counterpart the *Observer.* So I took the opportunity to ask the executives if my cost-cutting theory was correct. To my surprise, they said cost had nothing to do with it. They assured me that it was actually more expensive to print the news on large sheets of paper. But, like their peers at PCM, they had no clue why the large format was the format of choice in the industry.

Soon after, I decided I should try to find out where the large format had originated. I asked people at the *Guardian* and other newspapers, but I received the same answers. "It has always been like that," they told me, shrugging their shoulders.

Undeterred, I stubbornly asked two research assistants to join the cause. They interviewed even more people—at the *Times*, the *Financial Times*, and the *Wall Street Journal Europe*—but received pretty much the same reply: "Don't know. It has always been like that."

This time, I refused to take "I don't know" for an answer. I was convinced that there was a reason for the large format, so I sent the research assistants to the British Library to dig through old books, documents, and newspapers. One morning, they came into my office and told me that they had discovered that the practice had originated in London, in 1712. As it turns out, the English government had started taxing newspaper companies based on the number of pages they printed. As a consequence, newspaper publishers began printing the news on larger sheets of paper to avoid paying more taxes.

Although the practice made little economic sense after the tax law was abolished, most newspaper companies continued to use the broadsheet format for no other reason than the unproven belief that customers wouldn't want it any other way.

And here again is how a good practice transforms into a bad one: after time passes and conditions change, everybody keeps up with the practice because they don't remember why they started it in the first place. But there's a happy ending to this story. While I was working with the *Guardian*, the *Independent* launched a much smaller edition of its newspaper that was exactly half the size of its original and, as a result, its circulation increased.

Finally, someone had the courage to buck the trend.

A Striking Experiment

To be fair, the *Independent* had nothing to lose. Since it was on the verge of bankruptcy, it wasn't worried about alienating its customers as its competitors were. Desperate, its management team was willing to try anything.

There was a precedent, however. The *Metro*, a free paper distributed to commuters in big cities worldwide, adopted a smaller, magazine-sized format and quickly become popular among Londoners (including myself). The *Independent*'s editor, Simon Kelner, had observed the *Metro*'s success, and even though it wasn't a high-quality newspaper like the *Independent*, the *Guardian*, or the *Times*, he decided to give the smaller size a try. But first he ran an experiment.

Beginning in September 2003, Kelner began publishing the *Independent* in two formats in a small area northwest of Manchester: the traditional broadsheet and a compact version, exactly half its size. Apart from the difference in size, the newspapers were identical; the same stories, columnists, photographs, distribution points, timing of distribution, price—everything. When both versions launched, readers gravitated to the smaller format, which outsold the traditional format three to one.

Given its popularity, Kelner quickly decided to offer the small format in London, too. On the October 7, 2003, both formats were made available in the London market, and as was the case in Manchester, the smaller format was a success. In October alone, the paper's national circulation rose by 7.5 percent, even though the compact edition was limited to London and Manchester. After a month, Kelner decided to expand its reach throughout Britain. By May— much earlier than it had originally anticipated—the newspaper had abolished the broadsheet version altogether. In the following years, the *Independent*'s circulation rose by 20 percent annually, which was quite a feat in a shrinking market.

Customers really liked the smaller-sized newspaper, and not only commuters in the north of Manchester and London. As an executive at the *Guardian* put it to me, "An assumption all the newspapers had originally made was that the format was really of concern for commuters only. What we discovered was that even the non-commuters prefer magazine format."

Essentially, the editors and executives at the *Independent* saw the broadsheet format for what it was: a bad practice. By eliminating it, they created a new source of growth that their competitors, who were stuck in the past, hadn't foreseen.

Creating Something New

The tale of the giant newspapers offers various insights on how inefficient practices emerge and persist. But, more importantly, it also shows that identifying and eradicating bad practices can create a wonderful source of innovation.

This could mean adding a new product or a new wrinkle to an existing product—like smaller newspapers—but it could also simply concern ceasing a particular practice, like abandoning buyback guarantees in book publishing. Or it could mean altering the way you run your business, perhaps even altering something upstream that customers might not (or should not) even notice, such as outsourcing.

Perhaps it could mean creating a new business model. As I'll describe in the next two chapters, citizenM, a hotel chain, and Eden McCallum, a management consultancy, made the elimination of bad practices the central part of their business models. citizenM did away with the familiar trappings of mid-tier hotels. Eden McCallum shook up traditional practices by hiring its consultants on a freelance basis. Although both companies were new entrants, their founders were veterans of their respective industries who exploited bad practices to create something new and unique, and that makes them interesting case studies.

Then in chapter 7, I'll provide what I call "The Ten Commandments of Business Innovation" that, no matter how modest or grand your ambitions, will give you a framework for eliminating bad practices and creating something new.

CHAPTER 5

More Than Painting a Gray Wall Green

Rattan Chadha and Michael Levie, who had been introduced by a mutual friend, shared a common frustration: the hotel industry. Levie had managed large hotel portfolios for several international chains, including Sonesta and NH Hotel Group. Over the years, he had developed various ideas for innovative changes, but was often stymied by conservative hotel executives who were unwilling to experiment with radical ideas. Chadha was also fed up with the status quo. A serial entrepreneur and the founder of Mexx, an international fashion company that he sold to Liz Claiborne, Chadha was puzzled at how mid-range hotels remained so unsuitable for frequent travelers. Levie agreed, and he and Chadha decided to open up their own hotel chain that avoided most of the familiar trappings of more traditional hotels.

To Levie and Chadha, the hotel industry was relatively homogeneous and stable, and hadn't changed much since the onset of hotel chains over a half century ago. Which is true. For the most part, it doesn't matter what chain we choose: the amenities and experiences will be largely the same. We can choose between standard rooms and suites. We can expect a restaurant, a bar, and a lobby where the concierge and check-in desk are located, and perhaps a large room suitable for business meetings or weddings. On top of that, we're usually offered some extra, paid services, such as room service, films on demand, or spa treatments.

For Levie and Chadha, the homogeneity was stifling, and more important, it was holding the industry back from appealing to the tastes and desires of young people who travel frequently. Chadha had realized this when he was running his fashion company. "We had about 100 young designers who traveled to all the big cities for fashion shows and flea markets," he said in an interview.[1] "We didn't have the budget for them to stay in five-star hotels, and they didn't like the image of Holiday Inn. I wanted to create a hybrid: great style for a price a 25-year-old designer could afford. That concept existed in fashion but not in hotels."

Levie and Chadha saw a gap in the market and sought to exploit it. Along with their partners—Hans Meyer, a hotel development veteran; Campagne corporate strategist Klaas van Lookeren; and architect and interior designer Rob Wagemans—Levie and Chadha opened their first hotel in 2008 at Amsterdam Schiphol Airport, and a second in Amsterdam City in 2009. They called their budding chain citizenM, for "mobile citizens." They wanted to appeal to customers with a particular lifestyle: people who travel frequently to different cities, whether for shopping, business, or leisure, who are internet-savvy and happy to find their own way around, but who don't want to compromise on comfort and convenience.

The concept grew quickly, and in subsequent years, the group has opened up several hotels in London and in Paris, and one each in Glasgow, Rotterdam, New York, and Taipei. There are plans for further sites in Europe and the United States and a joint venture arrangement to roll out the concept to the wider Asian market.

The concept has been a great success and has garnered a long list of accolades. In 2008, citizenM won the Venuez Award for "Best Hotel Concept." A year later, the *Sunday Times* ranked it twenty-sixth on its "World's 100 Best Hotels" list, and CNBC ranked it fourth on its list of "Best New Business Hotels." In the same year, *Fortune* magazine placed it in its list of "The World's 50 Most Stylish Business Hotels." Subsequently, in both 2010 and 2011, TripAdvisor voted citizenM "The Trendiest Hotel in the World."

Something has worked, all right. The question is: how did Chadha, Levie, and their partners do it?

Innovation through Subtraction

Since Chadha and Levie had a specific consumer base in mind, they were able to develop a clear and concise strategy that guided every decision they made, from the design of their hotels to the services they provided. First and foremost, they identified the things that most hotels offered but that "mobile citizens" didn't need and eliminated them.

One of the first things they looked at was the check-in experience. Since their customers, who are young and mobile, are frequent travelers, the management team and designers streamlined the check-in experience to make it as fast and chore-free as possible. Instead of a large lobby with a check-in desk, citizenM installed check-in kiosks that dispensed keys in the same way as check-in machines at the airport, which their guests were familiar with. They also did away with hotel porters. Because customers were used to carrying their own bags from the airport, they could manage the last meters of the journey as well without assistance. This also made for a faster and frictionless experience.

The citizenM team also eliminated traditional restaurants, bars, and conference facilities. Business travelers usually travel alone, so they don't often sit at a full-service restaurant by themselves, and customers on a weekend trip would likely be eating out anyway. Instead, guests could grab prepared sushi or sandwiches from the fridge and cupboards in a small self-service room whose layout, lighting, and decor made it feel like a high-end home kitchen. The small footprint of the restaurant and absence of food prep on site had an additional advantage. Because space comes at a substantial premium in places like New York and London, the citizenM team could get more return on square footage while still allowing it to build its hotels in lively hot spots.

The citizenM team also revamped the public spaces. As you enter one of the hotels, you'll see one large downstairs space, loosely subdivided by trendy designer furniture and pieces of art, with a middle area referred to as "canteenM," which includes a bar area with a barista, where you can order coffee or a cocktail, and pay for the food you've taken from the "kitchen area." This appeals to customers who are on the go. For guests who want to stay in, there's a television, with the remote available to switch channels, high tables to eat or work at, and comfy sofas for reading or having a chat. The goal was to mimic the feel of a home—a luxurious, contemporary, open-plan home. Moreover, the team wanted the space to be so attractive that guests would prefer to spend their time in the open areas rather than in their rooms.

The bedrooms, therefore, are relatively small—the size of a shipping container. They are entirely manufactured off-site on an assembly line and transported in one piece to the hotel site. There they can be plugged in and stacked together in various shapes. "Just like playing Lego," Levie noted. The rooms are small but luxurious—a wall-to-wall double bed and a power shower—and full of technology in terms of lighting, music, television, and curtains, all operated by a single tablet computer. All of the guests' preferences are automatically stored in a central database, so that whenever and wherever they check in again at a citizenM, the preferences are immediately reinstated. Levie envisioned that guests would use the room for a good night's sleep, a shower, internet access, and perhaps film watching in privacy—all free of charge—but that when they got up, they would head down to the living room, just like at home. All this makes efficient use of valuable space and keeps costs down and guest satisfaction up.

citizenM's innovations weren't just customer-centric, however. The management team outsourced its on-site storage (linens, cleaning products, toilet rolls, etc.) to an outside company that cheaply stores those items and delivers them to the hotel each day. This practice economizes the space and makes room for more bedrooms. The internal organization of the hotel chain is also different from others. Inspired by retail chains, each hotel is operated by a small team of about five people, called "Ambassadors," who report to a one central support office. All of them are multitasking, instead of being assigned to one specific role, such as concierge, check-in desk, or waiter, as traditional hotels do.

Each Ambassador goes through an intensive six- to ten-week training program, and also attends workshops about creativity, local culture, and trust, and visits restaurants and other venues in order to learn about customer engagement. citizenM prefers to recruit people who have not worked in the hotel industry before, so that, as Levie put it, they haven't picked up any "bad habits." The main criterion is whether they can engage with customers. As one employee put it to me: "You can teach people how to make a mojito, but you can't teach people how to be nice."

Chadha and Levie also eliminated mass bookings; typically, hotels fill as much as 70 percent of their rooms long in advance for conference attendees, corporate clients, and airline personnel—at large discounts—leaving 30 percent of rooms for individual guests. Instead—just like low-cost airlines—citizenM prices all rooms in real time, dependent on supply and demand. Meanwhile, its construction costs are 40 percent lower than those for other four-star hotels, staffing is 40 percent lower, too, but occupancy rates (consistently above 95 percent) are considerably higher.

Note that Levie and Chadha realized that eliminating all these practices would not appeal to everyone. Some hotels, for example, fare well with restaurants and room service, and their guests wouldn't like it if these amenities weren't offered. The point is that these practices were antiquated in a particular corner of the market: the corner inhabited by frequent, well-seasoned travelers to large cities where space comes at a premium.

The citizenM team was able to create a seamless experience that catered completely to the needs of these customers. It didn't just paint a gray wall green, as Levie put it. It made the elimination of bad practices a central part of its business model and tailored every decision to the needs and wants of its specific consumer base. And, because of that, it has managed to innovate in a stable and homogenous industry, and ward off imitators. (See figure 5-1.)

When I visited citizenM in London Bankside, Levie and I walked over to a competitor hotel just around the corner, whose lobby was very similar to citizenM's. It

FIGURE 5-1

Three steps to break out in a tired industry

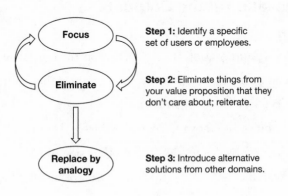

Focus

Step 1: Identify a specific set of users or employees.

Eliminate

Step 2: Eliminate things from your value proposition that they don't care about; reiterate.

Replace by analogy

Step 3: Introduce alternative solutions from other domains.

wouldn't surprise me if the competitor, as Levie alleged, had indeed sent an interior designer to the citizenM with the instructions, "We want one of those." There was a problem, though: it did not work. There was no buzz to the place at all. Very few people were in the space, which still felt like a hotel lobby with people checking into their rooms or quietly waiting to meet someone, all talking in subdued voices.

Their competitor had copied citizenM's "living room" space, but without the other practices in place, it all fell flat. Without the check-in machines, the multifunctional personnel, the internet marketing, the focus on frequent travelers, and so on, it was just a bunch of furniture in a green-painted space.

Innovation at the Output Side

citizenM's innovation is very salient on the output side: it offers a different customer experience altogether, and that is where Levie and Chatta's thinking began.

But business innovation can also start at the input side by eliminating bad practices on the other side of the market. By the "other side of the market," I do not mean what we usually think of when we think of "our market," namely, our end users, but input markets such as raw materials, supplier management, and, crucially, employees. I believe many labor markets are rife with terribly ineffective or outdated practices. In chapter 6, I give an example of a company that innovated by altering its business model for employees. Who knows, you might even decide to join it.

Innovation in the Market for Employees

Dena McCallum, who was the director of strategy at Condé Nast, was frustrated. The media organization—which owns *Vogue*, the *New Yorker*, and *Vanity Fair*—needed to change, but she didn't want to hire a management consultancy, as most companies do. As a former McKinsey consultant, she knew that a team of outside strategists would want to design and lead the program for her, something she was perfectly capable of doing herself. But she also knew that she needed help and wished she could hire a few former strategy consultants as freelancers.

That's when the idea hit her. For years, McCallum and her friend and ex-McKinsey colleague, Liann Eden, had discussed starting their own firm, but they couldn't settle on a good enough reason to leave their jobs. The freelance idea changed that. Although McCallum continued working for Condé Nast a while longer, the seed of an innovative plan had been planted.

In 2000, McCallum and Eden founded their London-based strategy consulting firm, which they proudly named after themselves: Eden McCallum. The firm would take on traditional consulting assignments, but it would operate unlike any other consulting firm: Eden McCallum would put no consultants on the payroll. Instead, all of them would work for the firm on a freelance basis. Eden and McCallum would secure the assignments and then staff them according to the project's requirements with people from their network of freelancers.

With a mixture of enthusiasm and apprehension, they set out to secure their first assignment.

"Growing Quickly and Zipping Upmarket"

Somewhat to their surprise, there were many consultants—from McKinsey, the Boston Consulting Group, or Bain—who wanted to work on a freelance basis for a variety of reasons. Some didn't want to work full-time anymore but wanted time off to travel, start their own companies, write a book, or spend more time with their families. Others wanted more control over which companies or industries they would be assigned to, while some wanted to work on projects that didn't require extensive travel.

More so, consultants were attracted to freelancing because it allowed them to do what they were trained to do—that is, consult. In traditional consulting firms, consultants basically have three roles: conducting client projects; acquiring new clients and projects; and helping run the firm, in terms of doing internal appraisals, being committee members, and managing functions. Some people really enjoy the first role—executing client projects—but do not like (or perhaps are bad at) the other two roles. Eden McCallum was happy to take them on; working for Eden McCallum, consultants were only required to fulfill the first role: execute projects to the best of their abilities. Eden McCallum's partners took care of the rest.

By 2015, Eden McCallum had grown to a team of seventeen partners and a pool of about a thousand freelance consultants: two hundred fifty worked mostly full-time, another two hundred fifty worked on one or two projects a year, and the rest worked sporadically. The firm had set up an office in Amsterdam and one in Zurich, with plans afoot to open up in New York too. Moreover, by 2015, its client list had grown to include a third of the companies in the FTSE100, a third of the world's largest private equity firms, and forty of the global *Fortune* 500 firms. Harvard professor Clayton Christensen wrote about it in *Harvard Business Review*, in an article on disruptive innovation in the consulting industry: "Eden McCallum . . . [is] growing quickly and zipping upmarket."[1] The model was working. Eden and McCallum had innovated in the consulting industry—an industry that had been stable and homogeneous for decades—not by giving customers something so very different, but by organizing itself in a novel way.

Changing "The Way We Do Things"

Do you work for a firm where managers think employees really have to work full-time? That forty hours per week (or whatever is considered full-time in your profession) is really a necessity? Perhaps you're one of those people with that conviction yourself—that, in your job, it is really not possible to work part-time.

I tell you, you're wrong: working five out of seven days is really just as arbitrary as working six days, or three— or twenty-eight for that matter. Chopping up the total amount of work that needs to be done in your firm into blocks that suit our human physiology has nothing to do with the actual work. If the total amount of work that needs to be done in a firm in one week equals twenty thousand hours, it is just as arbitrary to chop that up into five hundred forty-hour workweeks as it is to chop it up into eight hundred blocks of twenty-five hours. A five-day workweek consisting of eight-hour days happens to be the current social norm in many of our societies, but I have long thought that a company that disrupts this norm in its industry could potentially build a momentous competitive advantage out of it.

Eden and McCallum realized that seasoned consultants who were fed up with working slavish hours at McKinsey, Boston Consulting Group, or Bain could still deliver lots of value conducting client projects for three days a week, or eight months a year. They realized that consultants who no longer wanted to do internal work, as managers and committee members, or who were not very good at acquiring new assignments (but who were perfectly good

Innovate at the Input or the Output Side

In every industry, companies face at least two markets.

- The market for *end users*—customers, clients, or consumers (or whatever you call them in your line of business)
- The market for *employees*—the labor market

When firms seek to innovate, invariably they focus their efforts on the first market: the market for end users. However, the example of Eden McCallum shows that sometimes it is worth considering the other side of the market; sometimes a novel

at executing them), could still do a great job at working with clients.

This structure was not for everyone: there were ample management consultants who much preferred to be employed full-time at one of the traditional firms. But there was also a long line of highly qualified, well-seasoned consultants who found Eden McCallum alluring. As one of its consultants, Mike Brady, relayed to me: "It is a very

competitive advantage can be built by innovating in the market for employees. Starting from that side of the market, Eden McCallum found an inventive way to secure the most valuable resource of all: people.

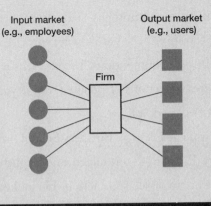

beguiling existence." Eden McCallum broke the traditional model of how a consulting firm can be organized. It had succeeded in innovating in an industry that had not really seen any innovation since its inception. This business innovation did not stem from giving customers something radically different, and that is where most companies start their thinking about innovation. The novelty came from the supply side: Eden McCallum had found an inventive way to secure the most valuable resource of all: people. (See the sidebar "Innovate at the Input or the Output Side.)

People Power

Most competitive advantages stem from people, rather than patents or products. I am always surprised when people find this point contentious, because this is what organizations are: collections of people (and, if you do it well, communities of people).

A colleague at London Business School—finance professor Alex Edmans—conducted an insightful study on the subject of employee satisfaction. He looked at companies that had made it onto *Fortune* magazine's list of Best Companies to Work For—an indication of high employee satisfaction. Subsequently, he looked at how the share price of those companies developed and found that it rose about 3.5 percent faster than others' did.

Edmans's research revealed two interesting things. One: it works. Employee satisfaction eventually translates into real, hard, financial value. Two: the stock market underestimates the effect of happy employees. That is because *Fortune*'s list is fully public; the stock market already knew the company had exceptionally happy employees, but it did not immediately factor this into the company's valuation. Only when—inevitably— the employees' happiness started to bear fruit in terms of the company's profits did the share price make a corresponding jump.

Hence, happy employees form a real competitive advantage, but investors—and, I bet, many managers—don't sufficiently realize that just yet. As the incisive management observer Henry Mintzberg noted, "Think of the organizations you most admire. I'll bet that front and center is a powerful sense of community."[2] Create a community in your organization, and you'll have created a competitive advantage.

Eden McCallum found a novel way to create a community of people tied to its organization, without putting them on the payroll. This formed the basis of its business innovation and enabled the firm to break into a market dominated by formidable and trusted brands such as McKinsey, the Boston Consulting Group, and Bain, whose reputations, networks, and relationships would have otherwise created formidable barriers. It then used this innovation to offer something a bit different to customers, too.

A Model That's Not for Everyone

When you hire a team of Eden McCallum consultants, what you get is not all that different from what you get when you hire one of the traditional consulting firms. After all, pretty much all its consultants spent years working for these firms. But there are a few differences.

Unlike the traditional firms, Eden McCallum does not really have a standard approach, in terms of the composition of the consulting team and the solution model it follows. Since all its consultants are independent freelancers, coming from slightly different backgrounds, it might have less common ground to build on, but its approach and solution are better tailored to the specifics of the client project.

Furthermore, Eden McCallum says that who you see is who you get. A common complaint about some of the traditional consulting firms is that the senior consultant comes in only at the beginning and the end of the project; in between, more-junior consultants do the actual work. At Eden McCallum, the senior consultants themselves execute the project. Moreover, in addressing another common complaint about traditional consulting firms, Eden McCallum consultants are preoccupied only with executing the project at hand, rather than with securing the next piece of work. Finally, given its low fixed-cost base, enabled by operating a network of freelancers, Eden McCallum is usually able to offer a substantially lower price than its more traditional competitors.

Are there disadvantages to this model? Of course; few things in life—including in strategic management—come with only advantages. Eden McCallum's approach is not for everyone. Some clients like it when the consulting firm comes in and runs the show; that's what they hire it for. Others have said that the Eden McCallum consultants feel "less like a team" than those from traditional consulting firms. That might be true, because they are all freelancers with somewhat different backgrounds. The global, standardized approach of a traditional consultancy is better suited to some projects and clients. And that's fine. Eden McCallum should not even try to appeal to everyone, just as citizenM is not trying to appeal to all types of customers. It should try to appeal to a specific group of clients and a specific group of employees. That's one directive for business innovation: "take aim at a chunk of the market." This includes the market for employees.

Eden and McCallum came up with their business innovation by eliminating the practice on the people side that everyone had to work full-time, conduct all roles, and be on the payroll. But, just as citizenM's hotels are not to everybody's taste and liking, Eden McCallum's model appealed to a good chunk of the labor market for consultants, but surely not to all. Similarly, its approach appealed to a group of clients in the market for consulting services, but not to all.

And that's how it works: when you're trying to innovate by shedding antiquated practices in a stable and homogeneous business, don't aim for the whole thing; find a (sizable) chunk in the market where you can shed some practices. Don't try to appeal to everyone. You'll end up serving no one.

As Levie of citizenM said to me: "I think that when you decide on a niche market, when you decide on what you want to be doing, do that extremely well and don't do other things. [Other hotels in] the industry create hotels that mid-week should be good for a business traveller. On the weekends it should be good for a group or a wedding party, or for a family. Good luck! It ain't happening. [You can't] create a boat that has an engine, is a rowing boat and a sailboat all in one. Decide who you want to be and be very good at it!"

Practices that are inefficient and discardable in one corner of the market can make perfect sense in another. Match your practices with your specific market and don't just do what others are doing. Both citizenM and Eden McCallum innovated in their industries by defining their chunk of the critical market (whether for customers or for employees) and, first and foremost, eliminated what didn't work or was superfluous.

It's the fit between the two that makes it work.

Let's now move on to the ten commandments of business innovation. These commandments will help you detect some of your own bad habits and reinvigorate your business by eliminating them.

CHAPTER 7

Ten Commandments for Identifying and Eliminating Bad Habits

The following commandments, which consolidate what we've covered so far, are a launching pad for some concrete recommendations on identifying and eradicating bad practices. If you're inspired to break a few bad habits in your own organization or industry—and I hope you are—these commandments will help you achieve your goal.

The Ten Commandments of Business Innovation

1. Cut out the benchmarking.
2. Reverse benchmark instead.
3. Experiment if you can (but make sure to do it well).
4. Monitor entrants and companies in distress.
5. Ask insiders for concerns.
6. Ask outsiders for suspicions.
7. Create bundles of practices.
8. Take aim at a chunk of the market.
9. Just stop it.
10. Watch out for "That's the way we do things around here."

1. Cut Out the Benchmarking

When we don't quite know what to do, we often do what others are doing and then feel safe and secure—just like sheep (or lemmings) in a herd. The formal term for this is "benchmarking." As discussed, benchmarking can be a real dud for innovation, and a wonderful way for a bad practice to spread and persist. Comparing yourself—in terms of practices or performance—with a group of self-chosen "peers" and then mimicking them is just an excuse not to think for yourself. So, cut it out.

Don't follow the herd, unless you thoroughly understand why their path is the right one. If you're just following the herd for the sake of it, you're going to feel pretty foolish as you plunge over the cliff with them.

2. Reverse Benchmark Instead

When it comes to opportunities for innovation, we usually think of fast-changing industries such as computer electronics, telecom, software, robotics, or gene technology, using the examples of Uber, Tesla, and Google. But I'm often inclined to think the opposite. Innovation through eliminating bad practices is more plausible in stable, homogeneous industries, where every firm does pretty much the same thing and in the same way.

There are many industries in which firms are scarily alike, often much more alike than the customers they seek to serve. There are many industries in which competitors are quite undifferentiated, and doing pretty much the same thing. It is in those industries where the opportunities are usually plentiful.

Look for a practice that almost everyone is using. Are all your competitors doing the same thing, like the broadsheet format that newspaper publishers preferred? If so, ask yourself if you understand why that is. Then ask others. If no one gives you a satisfactory answer, there could be a good opportunity for innovation.

That is what I mean by reverse benchmarking. By all means, assess what your ten closest competitors are doing. But if they're all doing pretty much the same thing, and if you cannot explain to yourself why all types of customers and employees are best served by that one approach, see if you can depart from the crowd. There's a good chance they were just suckers for success. There's a good chance this one way of doing things is an antiquated relic and, therefore, a disruptive innovation is waiting to happen.

In a way, this is exactly what Southwest Airlines did in the airline industry. Every established airline was—so to speak—serving three-course meals on a forty-five-minute flight. Its founder Herb Kelleher thought, "Why is that . . . ?" and changed it. It is also what Simon Kelner of the *Independent* did when he changed the size of the newspaper. Everybody else was printing broadsheets (and unable to explain why), and he just decided to do it differently. This reverse benchmarking won't catch all bad practices—in IVF, for example, executives can give very logical-sounding, gleeful (if erroneous) explanations for why selection at the gate is so advantageous—but it's a great place to start.

3. Experiment If You Can (but Make Sure to Do It Well)

When you make several changes at once in a complex system and subsequently observe the performance outcome, you have no idea what's really driving those results. So, as Kelner tested a smaller edition of the *Independent* in one corner of the market, you need to change one element and nothing else. That way, you should be able to understand the influence of exactly that element on your company's performance. This is the good way to run an experiment. The problem is, a lot of managers don't follow this method, and their results are compromised as a result.

The Good Way to Experiment

Kelner ran a genuine, controlled experiment. He changed the size of the newspaper in one locale, Manchester, and then another, London. But all other variables—newspaper content, distribution points, timing, and so on—were identical. When the smaller version then sold much better for several months, he could confidently conclude that customers preferred it because there was nothing else to peg the success to.

If your organization can run such a genuine, controlled experiment, it can be a great way to resolve the causal ambiguity that keeps a bad practice afloat. I realize that designing an experiment in an organization is not always possible. Even if you can, sometimes you have to run the experiment for quite some time to make sure you're not just capturing a short-term effect. But if you can design such experiments, they can be a great way to disentangle the complexity that otherwise slyly conceals a damaging practice.

The Bad Way to Experiment

There's only one thing worse than not running an experiment: running a bad experiment (but dressing it up as a proper one). I saw this clearly when talking to people in the pharmaceutical industry on the topic of "detailing," which is basically the way pharmaceutical companies (in most countries) do marketing: they send salespeople with suitcases full of their pills and ointments—and lots of free samples and other goodies—to physicians, to persuade them to prescribe their drugs to patients. Professors Natalie Mizik and Robert Jacobson—then at the Columbia Business School—did extensive research on the effectiveness of this practice and concluded that, despite pretty much everybody doing it, it is wholly ineffective. Specifically, they found that it requires, on average, no fewer than three visits and twenty-six free samples to induce a doctor to write just one new prescription, which doesn't sound terribly effective. However, the practice remains widespread. Mizik and Jacobson therefore pondered, "Why would the firms persist at engaging in a practice that has negative returns?"[1]

Detailing has all the hallmarks of a classic bad practice that was once effective. Started when fewer drugs existed and drug information systems (e.g., online databases) were more difficult for physicians to access, it made sense to send salespeople to doctors' offices with samples. But things have changed: the number of drugs on the market has increased exponentially, and doctors are more privy to data and information.

Yet detailing, as various people in the pharmaceutical industry whom I interviewed noted, has escalated to a level—in terms of the number of drugs being promoted, number of visits, and number of sales representatives—that looks excessive. For example, estimates are that during the 1996–2005 period, drug companies increased their sales forces by 42 percent, whereas productivity declined by 26 percent, something interviewees were aware of. "In many cases, the market has reached saturation," noted an executive at Novartis. "Companies are ramping up their salesforce, sometimes to irrational levels," an Amgen manager said. Thus, organizations may assume that detailing is a beneficial practice because in former times and at lower levels, it was effective.

Yet, various pharmaceutical companies also convinced themselves that it was an effective practice by creating a dubious association with success. For example, they would do internal research measuring whether there was a positive relation between the amount of detailing of a particular drug and its sales. Usually, this relationship was positive. As the manager at Novartis remarked, "Several [in-house] studies show a strong correlation between salesforce activity and actual firm sales." However, in this case, correlation by no means equals causation. Better-selling drugs would likely attract the attention of more salespeople, who would begin marketing it more heavily too. More-promising drugs—which generated particularly encouraging results in their clinical trials—would attract more enthusiasm and attention from the firm's sales force, while irrespective of this attention, also would generate more sales given their superior efficacy. In any case, the results of these internal studies might very well be misleading.

The Ugly Way to Experiment

One manager I spoke with (not among the interviewees quoted above) described how his firm had run an experiment with four of its drugs that had recently, and almost simultaneously, emerged from its R&D pipeline; the company launched two of the drugs with detailing, and the other two without. "And," he concluded, "the results clearly showed that the two with detailing performed better [in terms of sales]. It seems detailing still works."

However, when I probed him about the selection process, he admitted that the drugs it had brought to market without detailing weren't the most promising ones in its portfolio to start with. He explained that top management had not wanted to take any risks with the two very promising drugs in the R&D pipeline. After all, these drugs were earmarked to become the next blockbusters. Surely I couldn't expect them to mess about with these! Hence, the ex ante most promising drugs had been launched with detailing, while the least promising ones would form the group going to market without the practice. This clearly is a very ugly way to run an "experiment"; the company was stacking the odds against the products without the practice.

Such flawed findings strengthen the (erroneous) association of the practice with success. Once this experiment was conducted, the findings became an explicit reason for the company's management to continue with the practice and to suppress dissenting voices that argued against it. In the end, the manager said, "We just could not find conclusive evidence that the practice was not effective." Therefore they continued it.

If you're unable to run a genuine, objective experiment but can only run a flawed one, you're probably better off not running an experiment at all. The harmful practice will emerge victorious, stronger and more tenacious than ever.

4. Monitor Entrants and Companies in Distress

If you're unable to design a genuine experiment to test if certain strategies and practices are antiquated, the next best thing is to monitor new entrants in an industry and, perhaps even more paradoxically, companies in distress, only to see what they are "experimenting" with. Consider again the example of broadsheet newspapers. Yes, the *Independent* was the first established newspaper to go tabloid, but it wasn't the first real newspaper of that size in the industry. As said, the free, smaller-format newspaper, the *Metro*—an entrant into the business—had come in a few years earlier. And it did rather well. This also led the *Independent* editor Kelner to sit up and take notice. Although not a perfect experiment in the academic sense of the word, it provided lots of information.

The same goes for detailing in the pharmaceutical industry. For example, companies could have looked to Takeda, the largest pharmaceutical company in Japan. Although Takeda is hardly new to the business—it's operated for over 230 years—it has recently entered many European countries. As its UK managing director told me, whenever Takeda entered a new country market, it tended to do so without the practice of detailing in place. Like many others, it had been having doubts about the effectiveness of detailing for many years (if only because it is wildly expensive), and it was happy to enter a new market without it. In a new market, where it does not yet have a presence, it can't lose an established position by shunning the practice.

Entrants have little to lose, whether its market positioning or legitimacy in the eyes of doctors. There are no sunk costs. Emboldened by lower risks, they are more likely to abolish a practice and experiment with something new.

Companies that have even less to lose than entrants are, of course, companies in distress. That the *Independent* was the first traditional newspaper to switch to a tabloid format was no coincidence: it was on a clear path to bankruptcy and was willing to do just about anything in order to survive. The *Times*, on the other hand—which was doing relatively well in the same market—didn't experiment with a new format because it had much more to lose. But, after noticing that the *Independent* found success with a smaller format, its managers and editors decided to make the switch as well.

5. Ask Insiders for Concerns

There is an even easier way to uncover the bad, antiquated practices in your company or industry: ask employees. Sometimes when speaking to an audience of executives, I ask them to name a practice that has lived on at their companies for a long time that they, however, suspect is ineffective or even harmful. Everyone always has an answer.

This is very common; each of us has suspected that a practice isn't worthwhile. Many pharma managers had been discussing the dubious efficacy of detailing for years. Newspaper companies had been talking about moving to a smaller format for longer than they could remember. I have yet to meet a book publisher who does not think that buyback guarantees are antiquated and inefficient. Although employees may not be 100 percent sure if a practice is bad—how could they, without evidence?—they will have serious misgivings.

Your colleagues are likely harboring suspicions about a particular practice. So why don't you ask them? If they do voice concerns, I challenge you to ask yourself, "do *I* understand why we do it that way?" And if your answer is "because we have always done it that way" or "because everybody does it this way," then you should consider whether there might be something wrong with it and whether you might be better off doing it differently. Because usually when managers and executives can't explain the reasons for adopting a practice, something is amiss.

Asking employees for what they suspect might be bad practices is a great place to start. They may not be able to pinpoint a particular practice as bad, but you can still learn a lot from them. The doctors, pharmacists, embryologists, and hospital managers I talked with in IVF clinics, for example, didn't claim that selection at the gate was a bad practice or that it could lead to long-term competitive disadvantages. Like most on-the-ground employees, the workers at these clinics weren't positioned at a high enough vantage point to fully understand what was happening. But their concerns, if listened to, could have helped managers see the problems for themselves.

Employees understand the internal workings of their parts of the organization. Doctors in IVF clinics, for example, knew that selection at the gate was affecting their jobs. "I think those difficult cases teach us much better how to do our job, how to understand the real depth of infertility as a medical condition, how to acknowledge our ignorance in order to overcome it," one doctor told us. "If you don't let the *bad cases in, to teach you failure, to teach you pressure, you'll oversimplify, you'll miss many of the underlying causes.*"

Even though the employees—doctors and other medical personnel—could not oversee the macro pattern that would emerge from avoiding difficult patients, they did understand the micro consequences. They understood that clinics developed new insights and better internal communication patterns as a result of treating challenging patients. And from their insights, managers should have been able to piece the different parts together and develop an understanding of how ditching or adopting a certain practice might affect their firms in the long run.

6. Ask Outsiders for Suspicions

Whereas insiders may voice reservations, outsiders can raise suspicions. On a micro level, new employees can notice and challenge existing, flawed conventions. Newcomers can often more easily see what is wrong and what habits and practices are bad.

Most managers and executives readily agree that new-comers can challenge existing ways of doing things. In reality, however, new employees more commonly adapt to the ways of the organization than the organization adapts to their novel points of view. I recently gave a keynote speech at a large private bank—let's call it Acme—on this very topic. Afterward, an executive who was quite new to the bank approached me. She said, "I have noticed certain ways in which they do things that really make no sense, but they just won't listen to me! They just shrug their shoulders and say, 'That's the [Acme] way.'"

Her experience is, of course, quite common. Outsiders may notice flaws, but that doesn't mean someone will listen. Most of the time, dissenters don't even speak up. But even if they do, they are likely to be ignored. My advice to the Acme banker was to not speak up until she found someone who agreed with her, and then to speak up together. That's because research has shown that we don't usually listen to a lone voice of dissent, but we will respond to a small group.[2]

Organizations should solicit the suspicions of newcomers and encourage them to speak up. New voices are plentiful, especially in organizations that are actively recruiting and hiring. As a standard operating procedure, it makes sense to systematically ask recent hires about practices that might be detrimental, inefficient, and antiquated.

7. Create Bundles of Practices

The example of the giant newspapers represents a dichotomous choice: you have either a broadsheet newspaper or a smaller one. Many practices though—good and bad—come in bundles. This complicates things, but also can make your innovation more sustainable in terms of the competitive advantage it provides. If a bundle of practices forms a set of interrelated choices that fit together, in strategic management we tend to refer to it as a business model. Ridding bad practices often implies eliminating certain elements from the bundle that don't really belong anymore because they don't make sense for a particular group of customers (e.g., citizenM) or employees (e.g., Eden McCallum), thus creating a new business model.

citizenM, for example, unbundled the set of practices that traditional hotels offer by eliminating restaurants, bars, check-in desks, and so on—practices that its chosen set of customers ("mobile citizens") no longer required. By maintaining or boosting other practices that these customers did care about—for example, processes that bring convenience, comfort, and luxury—the company created a new business model altogether. That's what you should aim for when eliminating certain antiquated practices from a bundle: to create a new business model that represents a set of practices that do fit very well together.

Bundles Form Business Models

Business models have been a hot topic in academic literature and the popular business press for over a decade. They involve a number of operational choices that culminate in one overarching strategic decision, which differentiates one company from the next. For example, the business model of low-cost airlines is clearly different from that of traditional airlines. Low-cost airlines eliminated all frills (meaning no free newspapers, drinks, hot towels, let alone three-course meals onboard). They eliminated difficult network connections by flying point-to-point on short-haul routes only (meaning, for instance, that one airplane flies back and forth between London and Amsterdam all day). They standardize as much as possible, for example, by always using the same type of airplane. They eliminated travel agents by selling tickets directly to customers over the internet. They turn around their airplanes very quickly as soon as they land (often within twenty minutes) to not waste time or money while idling on the runway. Traditional airlines, by contrast, offer lots of amenities and connecting flights, often with alliance partners, and usually have a whole fleet of airplanes of different types, which they fly to primary airports in all sorts of locations. Both are airline companies, but they have very different business models.

Sometimes just one practice is bad and you can enhance the business model by altering this one choice (e.g., the size of your newspaper), but more often several practices are antiquated and the whole business model needs changing (e.g., the whole business model of your airline). The good thing about creating a new business model by eliminating bad practices is that it becomes hard for incumbents to emulate. That is because the practices fit together and will only work in unison. Traditional airlines won't gain much by only eliminating their onboard frills, if they don't concurrently shift to point-to-point short-haul flights, standardized aircraft, and direct sales (which is all easier said than done). Similarly, traditional hotels won't gain much by merely copying the style of citizenM's lobby (as one of its competitors did), without putting all the other practices in place. Hence, realize that practices seldom travel alone. When you are eliminating some bad ones, you should try to create a new bundle in the process.

8. Take Aim at a Chunk of the Market

Even though a practice can be universally and uniformly bad for every firm in a particular industry, sometimes the practice is only nonsensical in a particular part of a market but not in others. The erroneous association with success—which a bad practice needs to survive—can stem from exactly this: it leads to success in a particular corner of the market, although, unbeknownst to the firms in the industry, it makes no sense in another.

In discussing the second commandment—about reverse benchmarking—I stressed that a promising way to identify a bad practice is to look for an industry where pretty much everyone does things the same way. That is because the same practices are unlikely to be optimal in all corners of a market. What may be a good practice in one part of the market is likely a detrimental one in another. Identify a practice that everyone is universally using in your industry, and you will likely have made good strides finding one that is a bad practice in some chunk of the market.

This, of course, is basically what Southwest did in order to innovate in the airline industry. A no-frills model built on operational standardization and simplification is not superior in all parts of the airline market. In some segments, offering meals, frills, and network connections makes perfect sense and is not a bad practice at all. Similarly, as you have seen, both citizenM's and Eden McCallum's founders are explicitly aware that their business innovations achieved by altering bad practices are not for everyone and, to put it in the words of citizenM cofounder Michael Levie, "We're fine with that." They've identified a substantial corner of the market where the industry's long-standing conventions no longer made sense and they are thriving there by having eliminated them.

9. Just Stop It

Although it might seem that the two aforementioned points complicate matters—about bundles of practices and some practices being harmful only in parts of an industry—even in these cases, innovation is often as simple as stopping a practice that doesn't work. Stop selecting at the gate in IVF, stop offering buyback guarantees to book retailers, stop detailing in pharmaceuticals, and stop printing on expensive, large sheets of paper. Of course, I realize there are lots of ifs and buts to consider in each case, and there are various cognitive and relational constraints that may make it difficult to ditch them. Still, I maintain that business innovation through the elimination of bad practice sometimes is as simple as ceasing to do something that is harmful, inefficient, or overly expensive.

Southwest Airlines stopped offering frills, stopped maintaining complex network connections, and stopped complicating things by operating a multitude of airplane types. Its strategists innovated by eliminating unnecessary evils—ones that a large segment of customers don't really care about—which enables the airline to perform better on other dimensions (if only on price), rather than coming up with new, additional things to do. This is sometimes difficult for companies to admit and acknowledge, because when we talk about innovation, we tend to think first about creating and adding new things.

One reason the elimination of unnecessary evils can be a promising route to innovation is that organizations and whole industries are often inclined to "optimize" a particular variable too much for too long. This over-optimization can concern internal practices such as excessive cost-cutting, excessive standardization, or excessive customer selection (as in IVF), but can also include giving customers too much of something. Traditional airlines, for example, were piling so many frills on customers for so long that many of them no longer cared and would happily swap yet another hot towel for a lower price. Similarly, television manufacturers, in an effort to gain on the competition, have been creating TVs with sharper and sharper images, and have now resorted to boosting the size of the screens because the human eye wouldn't be able to detect the difference otherwise. Pharmaceutical companies have continued to push detailing despite the fact that most doctors are not responding to it any longer. This what the Novartis executive meant when he relayed that "the market has reached saturation" and the Amgen manager when he said that "companies are ramping up their salesforce, sometimes to irrational levels." Too much of a good thing still creates a bad thing. Cutting back or eliminating it altogether might serve you better.

If most companies in your industry are offering something that customers don't really care about anymore, you've probably discovered a bad practice.

10. Watch Out for "That's the Way We Do Things around Here"

Let me finish my lineup of commandments with what is perhaps the most prevalent symptom in the examples thus far: employees utter the comment "that's the Acme way" or "that's the way we do things around here" when asked about a particular practice. Whenever you hear that line, suppress a (premature) smirk but pay attention; you may have just encountered an antiquated habit.

The Monkey Story

In the 1950s, Gordon Stephenson was studying the cultural transmission of learned behavior through experiments on primates, most often rhesus monkeys. Stephenson was a biological psychologist, someone who tries to learn something about human behavior by studying other primates. One day—goes the story—he locked five monkeys in a cage, in the middle of which, on a piece of string, he had hung a banana. Underneath the banana, he had placed a ladder.

One monkey, whom Stephenson must have slightly underfed, ran hungrily toward the ladder. But when the monkey stepped in the first rung, he and the other monkeys were immediately sprayed with ice-cold water from a sprinkler, and he hastily retreated.

Soon after, another monkey tried to climb the ladder, but the same thing happened: he and the other monkeys were sprayed with ice water and retreated. After a few attempts, the monkeys got the message: banana or no banana, no climbing up the ladder in this place. From then on, they stared hungrily at the yellow delicacy but didn't dare try to remove it from its perch.

Then Stephenson made things a bit more interesting: he replaced one of the monkeys with a new one. Before long, this monkey, blissfully unaware of the evil sprinkler treatment, approached the ladder with a plan to climb it and get the banana, thinking, "Why have these suckers not grabbed it yet? Are they blind, or what?" The other monkeys, who knew what to expect, jumped up before the new guy could even get near the ladder, chased after him, and together beat him up.

Although shaken, this new monkey didn't give up immediately. But each time it strayed close to the ladder, the other four would bare their teeth or deliver a few well-aimed punches at the ignorant newcomer's head. After a while, this new monkey also got the message: banana or no banana, no climbing up the ladder.

Then Stephenson upped the stakes a bit further: he replaced a second monkey. This monkey, too, approached the ladder, but his cage mates jumped up and chased him. Interestingly, though, the first new monkey, who had no experience with or knowledge of the ice-cold treatment whatsoever, also jumped up, chased after the new guy, and with equal pleasure and enthusiasm, joined the beating.

Stephenson then replaced a third monkey, with the same effect; then a fourth one, and a fifth one, until all the monkeys in the cage had been replaced. None had experienced the ice-cold-water treatment (in fact, there was no ice-cold-water treatment anymore; Stephenson had long ago turned off the sprinkler system), but none of them dared to approach the ladder. Instead, they sat hungrily on the ground below, staring at the banana.

A Talking Monkey

Next, yet another new monkey was sent into the cage. This monkey also spotted the banana and with youthful enthusiasm hurried toward the ladder. Predictably, the other four jumped up, chased after him, and beat him up. But this new monkey raised himself off the ground, turned around, and proclaimed with indignation: "Why do you beat me up when I try to reach the banana?!"

The other four stopped, briefly glanced at each other, and after a moment of pensive silence, shrugged their shoulders. "Dunno. But that's the way we do things around here."

Perhaps not coincidentally, this is the textbook definition of organizational culture. You will probably find it in eight of ten handbooks on the subject, and probably on page one or two: "the way we do things around here." It's the Acme way. But if that's your explanation for why you do things, you might be willfully maintaining an outdated practice.

Since publishing this story—which I heard from my good friend and colleague Costas Markides—I have heard from quite a few people. It clearly hit a nerve. Evidently, it reminded many people of their own organizations. Perhaps it reminds you of yours too? If so, I suspect you may have just identified an antiquated habit in your firm.

Some of these people, however, also asked me, "Did this experiment really happen?" Frankly, I don't think that's very important. It's the parallel and recognition of how things work in your organization that matters.

Stephenson certainly existed and conducted experiments of this nature. He published quite extensively on the topic of the cultural transmission of learned behavior and the various animal experiments he conducted, although the ones I read about usually used blasts of cold air instead of water. Although I haven't been able to find an article by him on the particular experiment I described above—with five monkeys in a cage and a banana—it is quite feasible that he conducted it in more or less this way. Although I am still pretty sure there was no talking monkey!

Importantly, what Stephenson's work has shown is that monkeys indeed display this type of behavior. Apparently, other animals do, too. For example, one person who contacted me about it relayed that sheep display the same behavior when confronted with an electric fence. Animals, including primates and humans, copy behaviors from their predecessors without really knowing the reason for the behavior and why that behavior and those practices came about in the first place. Spotting the situation—and that the sprinkler system might have long disappeared—is important to breaking such antiquated habits, whether you're locked in a cage with your colleagues staring at a banana, or whether you're trying to innovate in your business.

So if you ever hear your colleagues say, "That's just the way we do things. It's the Acme way," picture them as a bunch of caged primates staring avidly at a distant banana. Then go ahead and grab it.

———————

Identifying and eliminating the bad practices in your firm is certainly a good idea and I much encourage you to do it. But, ideally, you wouldn't stop there. Ideally, you'd built an organization that constantly and automatically renews itself, shedding antiquated practices and embracing change. It requires you to carefully balance your current competitive advantages with developing new ones. That is the subject of part three of this book.

PART THREE

Reinvigorating Your Organization

CHAPTER 8

Embrace Change for Change's Sake

Identifying and then eliminating bad practices, as I discussed, can create new sources of innovation. But, if organizations want to be successful in the long term, they also have to avoid breeding and adopting new ones. To do this, managers need to create organizations that constantly reevaluate and renew themselves, thus maintaining a breeding ground for innovation. The process of constant renewal; creating new products, processes, and services; and bucking the status quo can create a potent antidote to inertia, which is what bad practices thrive on.

In other words, the elimination of bad practices shouldn't be a one-off process. Bad practices are likely to pop up again, and if your organization settles into a routine and grows stale and complacent, these new bad practices will do just as much damage as the old ones.

There is no one silver bullet for how to organize for continuous innovation. But there are several complementary processes that foster ongoing creation and renewal:

Embrace change for change's sake. Don't wait for trouble and decline, but make proactive changes to your modus operandi.

Make your life difficult. Deliberately include challenging products, customers, or markets in your portfolio of activities; they can offer a wonderful source of learning.

Balance exploration with exploitation. Get organized so that you strike a balance—and keep carefully monitoring this balance—between activities that further enhance and exploit your current competitive advantage and those that foster new ones.

Be varied and selective. By all means, create an internal environment where a thousand flowers can blossom, but make sure you also have some stringent processes in place that systematically kill off 999 of them.

I'll be devoting a chapter to each one of these processes, but first, let's dive into embracing change for change's sake, an idea that prompted a lot of *Harvard Business Review* readers to send me hate mail.

Genius or Lunacy?

In 2010, my good friends and colleagues Phanish Puranam from INSEAD and Ranjay Gulati from Harvard Business School and I published an article in HBR titled "Change for Change's Sake." The crux of the article was that we should change our organizations regularly and repeatedly, even if there isn't a pressing reason to do so. This set off a lot of people. I don't think I've ever received as much hate mail after publishing a piece as I did then (although "Steve Jobs: The Man Was Fallible" might rival it). When readers write to me, they usually begin their emails with "Dear Professor," but after "Change for Change's Sake" was published, they more often addressed me as "You Idiot":

"You idiot: I have gone through my third reorganization in four years now and you're telling me that
there is value to that?!"

"You idiot, another CEO, another corporate change
program; they're completely pointless!"

Their ire was palpable; even the mainstream press
picked it up. CBS organized a vote on its business website
asking readers to indicate whether the idea was "Genius?
Or Lunacy?" And I have to admit that lunacy won.

But here's the thing: we weren't arguing that all
change is good or that more change is always better.
What we argued was that a company needs to routinely
shake itself up, regardless of the competitive landscape.
Why? Because executives usually look for "an excuse" to
change their organizations—say, something in the external environment that allegedly necessitates change, such
as a new technology, new customer demands, different
competitors, or a changed economic climate—but by
the time they find a legitimate one, it's often too late for
the change to avert a financial and organizational crisis.
Changing for change's sake forces companies to be more
proactive.

Senior managers are understandably resistant to our pro-change philosophy. They want a clear and definable reason to make a change. They want to be able to say, "Because factor X has changed in our environment, we now have to change, too." There's nothing inherently wrong with this kind of argument; if something fundamentally changes in your business environment (for instance, rendering certain practices obsolete), you may indeed have to change, too. However, you shouldn't need this excuse. Even if you were in a perfectly stable environment (which you aren't), you would still have to change your organization every now and then, because there's value in the process of change itself.

As I've described, organizations never remain stable; they change over time. People begin to interact with a stable group of colleagues, processes become routinized, and particular functions and departments gradually increase in power and amass more resources. This leads to a set of well-known problems: the formation of silos, which many of you will recognize from your own firms; the deadening impact of routine, which gradually leads to rigidity and inertia within teams and organizations; and the emergence of entrenched interests, aka the inefficient escalation of the distribution of power within a company.

These destructive problems are sometimes slow to form, often difficult to notice, and create breeding grounds for bad practices to proliferate. But by adopting a pro-change mindset, even when change doesn't seem immediately advantageous, your organization can prevent these problems from taking hold and, in the process, become more adaptive and flexible.

Let's look at each problem and various solutions in more detail.

Busting Silos

In order to optimize communication and coordination, organizations group their people in various ways: by product, function, or geography. From there, they add one or two other dimensions to their structure, thereby creating a multisided matrix-type organization. They also may add a couple of additional overlays and often jot in a few "dotted lines" between various departments. As time goes on, however, the org chart looks more like a work of cubist art than a diagram of the organization, and few employees understand (or adhere to) it anymore.

Although these overlays, matrices, and dotted lines serve a purpose, they still do not solve all communication problems. Worse, informal networks—social networks of employees—often mirror the formal structure as employees tend to only interact with the colleagues with whom they work closely. As a result, the silos develop that we all vigorously complain about.

In order to avoid these tricky coordination problems and to take full advantage of both formal and informal networks, companies should pick one very simple structure and then regularly change it over time.

A Hypothetical Example

Consider the hypothetical, simplified organization displayed in figure 8-1, which at Time 1 has grouped its people in units based on function. All the engineers are together in one unit (regardless of what product they are working on), and all the marketers are in another unit (regardless of what product they are working on), and so forth. The firm has a classic functional structure that a lot of organizations use.

We call this the formal structure of the firm. What research suggests, though, is that the firm's informal

FIGURE 8-1

The formation of informal networks

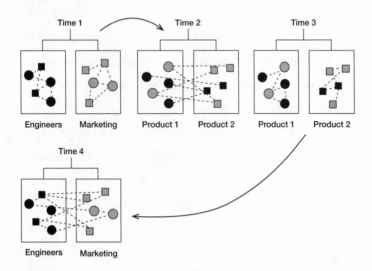

Solid arrows signify an organizational change or reorganization. Dotted lines depict informal networks.

organization—meaning its culture and the social networks—will gradually grow to resemble its formal structure.[1] Consider the informal network linkages between people in the firm. In the example in the figure, this alignment between the formal and the informal organization means that if the engineers go for a beer after work, they will do so with fellow engineers . . . and talk about the (strange) stuff that interests engineers.

Similarly, if the marketing people go for a drink after work, they will do so with their marketing buddies. As said, the informal network—displayed in the figure by the dotted lines—now perfectly overlaps the formal structure.

The problem with this is that it causes the emergence of the widely dreaded silos: people only communicate and coordinate with other people from their own unit. However, many problems—particularly the most crucial, pivotal ones—cut across unit boundaries, touching upon various functions and departments. Quality issues, misunderstandings of customer needs, innovation deficiencies, and various other potentially existential threats are hardly ever confined to the boundaries of one particular organizational unit. Hence, they require coordination across units. And this firm, at present, does not have it.

To avoid these problems, reshuffle these people into different units—as displayed in the example at Time 2— which will force employees to coordinate along different lines. All the people working on Product 1 (the circles), regardless of whether they are engineers or marketing folks, will now coordinate because they are together in a formal product department and will have joint meetings, a common boss, and so on. Similarly, all the people working on Product 2 (the squares) will also coordinate through these formal channels.

The advantage of this is that coordination now happens within *and* across units. All people working on one particular product will now coordinate along formal lines, while coordination across units (with colleagues in the same function) happens through informal channels.

The beauty of informal networks is that they do not dissolve immediately after you change the formal structure. If, for example, an engineer from the unit for Product 1 goes for a drink after work, he will regularly do so with his old engineering buddies, now in the unit for Product 2. And when they sit at the bar with a pint of Guinness, they will talk about stuff that interests (only) engineers. It's quite possible that some of them will proclaim, "Hey, that problem you guys are now dealing with in Unit 1 is exactly the same as we already solved in Unit 2; let me tell you . . ." By changing the organization, the firm gets the best of both worlds: people coordinate along product lines through the formal organization, but also along functional lines due to the old linkages of their informal network. Hence, the informal organization complements the formal structure.

Keep in mind that informal organizations don't last forever; people lose touch, people change jobs, people die, and so on. So, gradually—as displayed in the figure at Time 3—the informal networks will once more begin to overlap with the formal structure. The engineer will now no longer go for a drink with his old engineering buddies, but he will join the marketing colleagues from his own unit and talk about departmental stuff. The informal organization no longer complements the formal one. The solution then, I say, is as elegant as it is simple: change back to the old functional structure.

Engineers will once again talk with other engineers (about the weird stuff that gets engineers excited) because they have departmental meetings and a common boss; the same goes for the marketing folks. Yet, they'll still know the marketing people from the old days of the product units, so they can still coordinate about the joint product they're both working on—as displayed in Time 4. By changing a simple organizational structure periodically, you can have the best of multiple worlds, and let the informal organization compensate for the shortcomings of the formal one.

A Real-World Example

My friends Puranam and Gulati spent much time interviewing people at Cisco. Cisco makes products that enable data transfer in computer networks, including the internet. They can be found in most large, private and public organizations worldwide. In the late 1990s, Cisco was organized along customer lines, in the sense that its formal structure consisted of three semiautonomous groups that each focused on a particular customer type: internet service providers, large enterprises, and small-to-medium-sized businesses. Each group developed and marketed its own products to its customers. Alongside this formal structure, the company's culture had also evolved to be very customer-centric.

There's nothing wrong with customer-centricity, of course. But Cisco began to experience some typical silo problems. In particular, customer divisions were doing a lot of the same work, which led to inefficiencies and people trying to reinvent the wheel. As one executive, whom Puranam and Gulati interviewed, remarked: "If there was a (customer) problem, we'd get whatever resources were required to fix it and then execute on it, quickly. But the problem was that ten people would be doing the same thing across the company ten times over, at ten times the cost. And they'd get it done quickly, probably in about one-tenth the time that we do now, but it was just incredibly inefficient." So what did Cisco do? It got rid of the old organizational structure and made a new one, with groups organized by technology (rather than by customer). Now one group was focused on operations engineering (regardless for which customer); one group on all network management services; one on internet switching and services; one on optical; one on storage, and so on. The firm no longer duplicated technology solutions for each customer type, but grouped all people who worked on a particular technology together. This greatly improved efficiency.

Yet, employees working on the same customer accounts still had to coordinate with each other. But, now, these people communicated through informal networks. Consider the following quote from an executive whom Puranam and Gulati interviewed, speaking about coordinating with colleagues from different technology groups: "We have been working together for a lot of years, the engineers and the marketers know each other really well . . . this helps now, and there are a fair number of collaborations that go on across the business unit, even across technology groups. You can always pick up the phone and find someone on a certain project that you might have had a relationship with in the past."

This engineer explained how he would still get in touch with people—his former colleagues from the old customer units—to discuss customer-specific issues. If a client was uncomfortable with a particular Cisco product, people from different technology groups working on that account would coordinate informally to have the problem solved as soon as possible. They were able to do that so seamlessly and swiftly because their previous relationship in a department enabled them to approach one another.

Tellingly, several years after the reorganization—as predicted earlier in the hypothetical example—Cisco noticed that this customer coordination through the informal organization no longer happened as automatically as before, probably because the informal networks had gradually faded. In response, Cisco partly switched back to a customer structure by implementing "business councils," which replicated the old grouping by customer type. By switching back and forth, Cisco found it got the balance right.

The Deadening Impact of Routine

Organizations spend a lot of time and effort building, improving, and extrapolating value from a particular competitive advantage. This leads their processes and systems to become more efficient and more reliable. As far as short-term profits are concerned, these efforts to further enhance and exploit one's advantage are a good thing. But research has indicated that, over time, as firms concentrate fully on getting better at the one thing they're already good at, they are less inclined to pursue new sources of value and competitive advantage.[2] To put it bluntly, these organizations become deadened by routine.

One way to prevent inertia from building up is to restructure your organization in some way. By restructuring, I don't mean some sort of euphemism for firing people, but literally changing the structure of the formal organization. That is, regularly change the way you group people, the performance review system, the cross-functional groups, the company's remuneration system, the budgeting cycle, the structure of people's incentives, the appraisal processes, and so on.

The advantage to such regular changes: It forces organizations to practice changing. Change is a capability you need to develop and hone. You either use it or lose it. And, if you use it, and continue to use it, you'll be better prepared to make big and substantial changes when the time occurs.

Change Is a Capability

Suppose you have two identical firms that are confronted with a significant change in their external environment that they really have to adapt to by altering their formal organization. Firm A has not changed its architecture in

A Regimen for Change

Companies that change even before they have to don't undergo the painful, wholesale reorganization and restructuring that characterize many large firms. It's important to vary the focus of periodic change initiatives by choosing a different category—structure, rewards, or processes—and zeroing in on a different aspect for each round of change.

Structure

How is your business organized?

- Function (such as R&D, marketing, operations)
- Geography
- Customer type
- Product

a decade; firm B has made many changes to its structures and processes over the years. Which of the two do you think will find it easiest to adapt to the significant external change? The obvious answer is firm B.

If your organization changes regularly, changing will become easier. It's just like training for a sports event, musical

Rewards

What is emphasized in appraisals and remuneration?

- Individual, team, or companywide incentives
- Open versus confidential appraisals
- Short-term performance versus long-term development
- Revenues versus value-added

Processes

How do you carry out your work?

- Decision rights (who decides what; reporting lines)
- Distribution (centralized or decentralized)
- Location (which processes sit next to each other)
- Focus (customer or product)

piece, or dance competition: practice makes perfect. It prepares you for when it really matters: your championship game, concert, or performance. And organizations are no different. If a certain firm hasn't changed how it operates for a decade, but now suddenly it has to adapt to a significant external event, it will find changing its ways very difficult. By contrast, firms that have had quite a bit of training in (small-scale) change processes beforehand will find making a significant change when needed much easier to accomplish.

Change is a capability. The more you do it, the better you'll get at it, and the more prepared, proactive, and agile you'll be if an unexpected event occurs. For example, see the sidebar "A Regimen for Change."

A Serial Changer

Al West is the founder and CEO of SEI Investments, a fund of fund managers that manages about $650 billion, that is, a lot of peanuts. One of my executive MBA students at the London Business School, who worked for him, described him to me as a "serial changer": He was always mucking about with SEI, changing it in one way or another. I thought, that's a guy I need to talk to.

When we met at his office, West told me that he changed the organizational architecture of his firm so often that he often made his employees nervous. "Why are you always changing a winning team?" they'd ask him. "Why are you always changing the organization although it is working fine?" West's answer was simple and direct. He changed the firm because he wanted to ensure its continued success in the future. For West, improving SEI's capability to change allowed him, his partners, and his employees to "quickly change strategic direction, to seize new opportunities, or respond to new threats. In a world in which the business environment can change overnight [it] gives SEI the flexibility and the mindset to transform itself just as quickly."[3] Put another way, the "unnecessary" changes that West was making were preparing SEI to make more important and crucial changes when necessary.

When we spoke in London, West had just changed the way the company evaluates and rewards its employees, focusing on team-based incentives rather than individual ones. Or maybe it was the other way around; I forget. It doesn't matter because West changes the system every few years.

> "Do you think you will ever get it right?" I asked him.

> "No . . . of course not," he responded. "There is no one incentive system that solves it all."

The constant changes to the incentive system encourage his employees to have multiple perspectives on their jobs and hence be more well-rounded. Team-based incentives, or even companywide ones, make employees think beyond their own roles, be more willing to collaborate, and be more cognizant of the company's goals and mission. Once— after a year or two or so—they'd adapted and developed a bigger-picture mindset, West might change them back to individual incentives to reorient them to their own specific roles, or he might come up with something new altogether. There is no single perfect system—all have advantages and disadvantages—but if you alternate between various types regularly, employees will become more attuned to each.

That is the idea of change for change's sake: regular changes prevent rigidity from setting in—in the organization's processes, its culture, and people's mindsets. But, as is often the case, change is also a question of power.

Power Escalates

At London Business School, our professors are organized, as in any top business school, along functional lines: I am in the strategy and entrepreneurship department, but we also have an economics department, an organizational behavior department, a marketing department, and so on. The most powerful department within the school is finance. It gets, by far, the most resources: there are more finance professors than any other, they get paid more, they teach fewer hours, and so on. Rightly so, I say. Really. Finance is an extremely important department within our school, if alone because London harbors the biggest banking cluster in the world (i.e., "The City"), and hence many of our students find employment there. Therefore, since finance is so vital to our school, one can make a good argument that it should get more resources. But there is also a problem. More resources leads to more power, which leads to more resources, which leads to more power, which leads to more resources—you get the picture. Power has a tendency to escalate.

The more resources a particular unit acquires, the more it *can* acquire. For example, the most pivotal internal institution with London Business School is our appointments committee. A top business school such as ours operates more or less like a partnership, just like many consulting firms such as McKinsey. Instead of "partners," we refer to them as tenured professors, basically professors with a lifelong employment contract. All these tenured professors together form this institution called the appointments committee.

The appointments committee is called this because we—tenured professors—collectively decide who else will receive tenure, that is, who else becomes a partner in the school. Because finance is so very important within our school, more tenured professors are on this committee than anyone else. And, when we're hiring new professors, guess which ones finance professors usually vote for? More finance professors. Which means that the next year, even more finance professors are on the committee. And whom do these new colleagues vote for? More finance professors.

I am simplifying (but only a bit), but this is basically how the interplay between power and resources works. Resources are usually unevenly distributed within an organization; not all departments, functions, and people receive the exact same proportion of resources. There's nothing wrong with that; some functions or units are just a bit more important to the survival and prosperity of a particular organization than others. But because resources lead to more power and vice versa, the skewed distribution of power escalates and ultimately becomes wildly inefficient.

Research on budget allocation processes—for example, by Stanford University's Jeffrey Pfeffer—confirms these processes.[4] An organizational unit's power may at first accurately reflect its importance, but it tends to escalate when the power the unit has gained—owing to its importance—is used to obtain an even larger chunk of the company's resources, leading to structural flaws and inefficiencies. Activities that are not in the direct interest of any of the organization's most powerful group will not get done or will get done half-heartedly, customers will be dissatisfied by the company's performance in all but its core functions, and the best people who are not employed in any of the firm's central groups will leave for competitors. The company may be better off assigning a larger proportion of its budgets elsewhere. The only way to address such an antiquated power distribution—which, by sheer definition, implies taking away valuable resources from the most powerful—is to break it.

Not the Old Structure

Reorganization can break up outdated and inefficient power structures that otherwise are misdirecting a company's resource allocation. Such a reorganization needs to alter the dimension along which resources are allocated.

West, for example, told me that he had initially organized his firm into three divisions, each run by a director. But, after a while, West realized that some of the objectives he wanted to accomplish weren't getting done. Why? They didn't dovetail with the particular interests of his directors. He did not divulge too much, but I imagine that he and his three division heads would discuss matters, West would emphasize how important it was that these received appropriate attention, they would nod agreeably, and subsequently nothing would happen. Eventually, West said, he realized that the only way to make sure these tasks got done was to alter the structure of the organization itself.

West reshuffled SEI's three divisions into five competency units. Why five? It didn't really matter. It could have been seven units, or four, or some other structure altogether; the important thing was that the old structure ceased to exist. To make sure things changed, West had to change the entire structure of the firm and, in the process, change how resources were allocated.

As West was well aware, when the structure of an organization is causing a problem, you need to fundamentally change the structure itself, rather than patch it up. Otherwise, the problem won't be solved.

Frequently Asked Questions

Since writing "Change for Change's Sake," I have received many questions and statements. Here are the most common ones, along with my answers.

- Are there no costs to this?

- Do you really think you should change as much and as often as possible?

- What if we can't reshuffle people?

- Is this not difficult to explain to employees?

Are there no costs to this? Yes, there are! Organizational change is costly. It requires ample management attention; it makes people rather inwardly focused for a while; and it disrupts daily operations (which, in fact, might be the whole purpose of the exercise). But you're sure to face those costs at some point anyway.

Change is inevitable. But if you wait for your business performance to become untenable before you change, the total costs will be even greater because you'll be in crisis mode. So, yes, organizational change will be costly, but a proactive approach is less costly than a wait-and-see approach.

Do you really think you should change as much and as often as possible? No. You can change too much or change too soon. For example, if the engineers are still going for a beer with their old engineering buddies—who are now in a different product unit—I wouldn't change a thing, because the formal and informal organizations have not yet begun to overlap. Changing the formal structure again would be useless and counterproductive.

More is not necessarily better. But don't wait for problems to escalate: change before things have become untenable.

What if we can't reshuffle people? It's true that one particular structure just makes sense for some organizations, and that reshuffling people from product to functional or geographic groups doesn't make sense. At London Business School, for instance, we wouldn't group professors by anything other than topic area (such as finance, marketing, and organizational behavior). But these types of organizations can still adopt a change-for-change's-sake mentality.

Change for change's sake is not just about reshuffling people. It's about getting different people to interact with one another, creating new patterns and mindsets, unleashing innovative ideas and approaches. SEI's West, for example, made serial changes to his organization, but rarely did this involve reshuffling people. I imagine that, for a healthy organization, change for change's sake implies frequent changes to the less encompassing and invasive aspects of the organization's architecture (such as its remuneration system) and perhaps only once every few years a substantial alteration of the structure itself.

Is this not difficult to explain to employees? I asked this exact question of West, who acknowledged that it's difficult to convince people of the need for change when the company is performing fine.

Sure, it's easier to convince your employees of the necessity for change when you're in the river Styx and bleeding cash, but that doesn't mean it's wise to wait for that scenario to happen. It puts an extra onus on top management to explain that change is needed, even though the financial results are still fine, and there's no way around that. West also added that although the first few changes were difficult to explain, his employees eventually learned to expect change and accept—and gradually even appreciate—that "change is always happening here; it is part of the fabric of SEI."

Of course, not everyone is infatuated with change, and some people may leave. But that's OK. For change to be a key part of an organization, employees need to embrace it as part of their daily work, according to West. If there are people who don't accept and embrace it, then they probably aren't suited to work in your organization.

Is It Time for a Change?

I'm including a tool or questionnaire to distribute to employees in various parts of and levels in the organization. (See figure 8-2.) It will help you decide whether it's time to bring change to your organization and to help you determine roughly where you want to change things and how, depending on the specifics of the problems you're experiencing.

The tool is simple—more of a systematic guideline of what questions to ask. It builds on the assumption—that I most definitely believe in—that people within the organization often have a very good sense of the pressing problems and the symptoms, and whether it's time for a change.

FIGURE 8-2

A corporate cholesterol test

Distribute this questionnaire to all your managers occasionally. Respondents should answer with a simple yes or no. To ensure honest answers, preserve the respondents' anonymity.

The quality of communication and collaboration	Do employees interact only with people from their own group?
	Are there strong subcultures that align with business groups or divisions?
	Are there breakdowns in communication caused by the formation of silos?
	Has collaboration between groups decreased over the past five years?
	Category total of "yes" answers
The capacity to adapt	Is the organization slow to react to opportunities and threats in the market?
	Do people and groups operate according to well-established routines?
	Has it been a long time since your firm developed a significant new revenue stream?
	Has the percentage of revenue from new streams decreased over the past five years?
	Category total of "yes" answers
The balance of power among groups	Do influential groups or individuals use most of the company's resources?
	Is it difficult for people outside of the company's central group to obtain resources?

(*continued*)

Do influential groups or individuals impede decision making?
Have the groups or individuals that were influential five years ago extended their influence?
Category total of "yes" answers

Grand total of "yes" answers

0–2 "yes" answers: There's no need for change just yet.
3–7 "yes" answers: It's the perfect time for a change.
8–12 "yes" answers: You're late already; your company needs substantial change.

Don't treat it too dogmatically, though. It's a guideline to aid your own thinking and internal investigations, not a substitute for thought. You'll still need to apply your own good judgment for it to work.

You'll recognize the three parts of the questionnaire, which correspond to the three types of organizational problems discussed earlier. "The quality of communication and collaboration" corresponds to the problem of silos; "the capacity to adapt," to the notion that change is a capability, which you need to build up by doing it; and "the balance of power among groups," to the problem that the distribution of power and resources tends to escalate.

For each of the three problems, there are questions to ask your employees in various parts of the organization. For each problem, the first three questions are designed to diagnose the problem, and the fourth question to determine whether things are getting worse.* For each subsection, simply add up the answers and see how many "yes" answers and "no" answers you have gathered. At the bottom of the test are three scores to compare yourself to. A high score means, "You're late already; your company needs substantial change" (or will die trying). The middle score means "It's the perfect time for a change" (you're not in real trouble yet; if you change now, you just might avoid it).

There is also a category for low scores. This one means, "There's no need for change just yet." If you scored low, don't make a change. It would be ineffective, unnecessary, and probably even harmful, since you probably don't have real problems yet with silos, escalating power structures that impede resource allocation, or organizational rigidity. Changing your organization now would be too soon. Please continue as is.

Every organization is unique and exists within unique circumstances. Therefore, no tool will ever be generally

---

* I replaced one item from the version of the tool originally published in *Harvard Business Review,* namely, the item "Are many people uncomfortable with change?" I did this because when people started using the questionnaire, that item clearly did not work. Somewhat to my surprise, but in hindsight understandably so, people tended to answer no to this question, especially when their organization was in trouble. What they usually meant was "No, we're not afraid to change! It is not us. Please change—now (we're sick and tired of these problems)." Therefore, I replaced it.

applicable or substitute for your own judgment and thinking. It's not as if you will ever be able to press "Enter" and then see an answer roll out, explicating what you need to do in managing your firm. If that were ever possible, you (and I) would be out of a job pretty soon, to be replaced by an Excel spreadsheet. The tool is intended to help you think for yourself and to make a more systematic and sound judgment call about when to change for change's sake. If you're ever offered a management tool that claims to do more than this, throw it away (and use mine instead).

Closing Observations

I'll finish with a quote from the former CEO of Appex Corporation (later acquired by EDS). His statement is a bit extreme, but he got the gist of the argument and behavioral mechanism exactly right. He said, "Every six months, by design I change the organizational structure. I changed it in January; I'll change it again in June. We're growing at 10 percent a month. I feel when a company has grown 50 percent, it is time to change."

He added: "An organizational structure becomes a tool you're using to create a balance between conflicting modes of organizational behavior, such as flexibility and consistency. Each structure emphasizes one type of behavior and deemphasizes another. By continuing to change, you can balance the needs of the organization."[5]

The trick he understood well, of managing an organization with complex needs, is to create a balance between conflicting modes of organizational behavior, such as exploitation and exploration; long-term versus short-term objectives; a focus on individual performance versus companywide incentives; and so on. No one organizational solution ever solves it all. By picking one but changing it regularly and proactively over time, you can get it about right.

CHAPTER 9

Make Your Life Difficult

Organizations are naturally inclined to routinize things, and that isn't necessarily a bad thing. Through experience, they develop stable ways of working that coordinate and combine the efforts of various people and specialists. When an IVF clinic follows the standard protocol for a regular patient, for example, everybody knows exactly what to do and when, and the organization executes this task without much effort or disruption. It makes production fast, efficient, and reliable. Obviously, there's nothing wrong with fast, efficient, and reliable. But if you want to innovate, you'll need to disrupt this routine, and develop new solutions and new ways of working.

To put it bluntly, your team needs to makes its own life difficult. This is exactly what IVF clinics did when they didn't turn away difficult cases. By treating patients with complex etiologies, they experienced more valuable learning opportunities than if they concentrated exclusively on higher-probability cases. By experimenting, reflectively communicating about the results, and codifying their newfound knowledge—the three critical components of team learning behavior—the clinics were able to improve their practices in the long term.

Let's look at each component, one by one, in the context of the IVF industry, while exploring how your organization can increase its own learning behavior.

Exploration and Experimentation

You can't innovate without ever trying something new. This may sound quite obvious—and, frankly, it is—but many organizational processes and practices are precisely aimed at not doing this. Process management techniques (such as ISO 9000 or Six Sigma), for instance, are aimed at making processes more reliable and secure. In general, organizations are inclined to try to rule out variability and instead concentrate on what works best.

Organizations can find a great source and stimulus of experimentation in deliberately taking on difficult cases: products, customers, or projects. That's because for those cases, the standard solutions won't work, and thus organizations are forced to try out new things. Consider how it works for IVF clinics.

Treating patients with a complex underlying etiology and, hence, poor ex ante chances of success makes the life of a clinic quite difficult for a few reasons. For one, standard procedures usually don't work for these women. IVF treatment requires a sequence of several medical steps, and clinics follow protocols on how to execute these steps: what medicine to take, how much, precisely when, what tests to run, and when to perform what procedure. These steps are standardized. But when the standard procedure does not work, doctors, embryologists, and pharmacists are forced to experiment.

One doctor explained:

> What you see in the textbook or in the code of practice are treatment coordinates for standard cases,

the typical patients showing up for consultation, young couples under 35, with good egg reserve, good sperm, and good health. We have a lot of experience with them and they're easy cases where we rarely deviate from the standard procedure. And that's all fine, but when you get a difficult case, with complex pathology, and the standard procedure simply doesn't fit, what do you do? You change the practice, you start tinkering with the parameters, adding new things, adjusting doses and sequences so that it fits.[1]

He explained that when he and his colleagues encounter a challenging patient, they are forced to explore different solutions and develop new procedures. But then he added something even more important: "You start tinkering with the procedure for the easy case as well; you take what you've learned from that difficult case to the easy case."

And that is an important point. He explained that by itself, treating a difficult patient might not be very attractive and profitable: it simply is a lot of work and takes a lot of time, and it's not as if a difficult patient pays much more than a standard patient. But by forcing themselves to do complex cases, the doctors experiment and develop new knowledge. And that new knowledge also makes them better at treating the more straightforward, standard patients.

Similarly, an IVF consultant we also interviewed stated, "I think those difficult cases teach us much better how to do our job, how to understand the real depth of infertility as a medical condition, how to acknowledge our ignorance in order to overcome it. If you don't let the bad cases in, to teach you failure, to teach you pressure, you'll oversimplify. You'll miss many of the underlying causes."

Difficult cases may not seem very attractive at first sight, and you may even be inclined to shun them (as many IVF clinics do), but in the long run, they may help you explore and develop new ways of doing things, which will likely also benefit your more standard products and cases and, in the long run, your bottom line. It will also make your entire organization better and more innovative.

What Is Your Rally Car?

Some companies in some industries do this deliberately. Various car companies, for example, have rally racing teams. Rally racing is a form of motorsport that, unlike

NASCAR or Formula One, takes place on open roads that are often unpaved. Car companies such as Ford, Subaru, and Mercedes partake in rally races not only to increase their brand awareness or profits, but because the races provide challenging situations that aren't present in normal road conditions. In other words, they present opportunities for innovation. Many of the modern inventions in our sedans, sports cars, jeeps, and, yes, even our minivans had their genesis in racing: disk brakes, direct shift gearboxes and clutchless manual transmissions, push-button ignition, and various improvements to materials, suspensions, and tire technology have all come from racing. Even the humble rearview mirror originated from a race car.

Whether you are a car company attempting to win a race, an IVF clinic debating whether to admit a difficult patient, or a law firm deciding which suspects to defend, it is worth asking how much you might be learning from these opportunities. They might not seem profitable by themselves, but if they help you to experiment and explore new solutions, these might just have ample value beyond their direct use.

Most managers, I believe, would agree with this point, but when push comes to shove, they find it difficult to

keep doing things that may not show up on their balance sheets.

Some years ago, for example, I spent some time with a company making wound-care products. Its senior managers were always deliberating whether to scrap certain specialty products from their portfolio, which were aimed at very complex types of wounds that few patients in the world suffer from. Their argument was that the products were simply unprofitable; they were expensive to make and there were few customers. In the end, however, management decided against scrapping the product line, and I think it might have been the right choice.

It is difficult to measure—just as the long-term consequences were difficult to measure in IVF clinics—but these products might have been the company's equivalent of race cars. The solutions it had to develop to treat complex wounds might very well have enhanced its capability in creating products for more standard ailments as well.

So whenever you find yourself in a similar conundrum, realize that there might be big benefits to making your life difficult every now and then. I urge you to ask yourself, what is the rally car in your portfolio? Because my guess is you could use a rearview mirror too.

Reflective Communication and Coordination

It's probably not a revelation that the learning cycle requires exploration, in the form of active experimentation. But new ways of working, and new routines, do not emerge automatically. So people need to come together and jointly reflect on the outcomes of an experiment and engage in a process of sense making: Did it work? Why did it work (or not)? Could we do even better? How do we adapt our tasks to each other?

As one interviewee who works in the IVF industry told us: "The effort of treating such patients—and patients with poor prognosis in general—intensifies the interaction among our doctors, embryologists, and nurses."

When clinics take on difficult cases, they often need to deviate from their normal routines and procedures. Without a standard protocol, doctors, embryologists, pharmacists, and nurses have to find new ways to coordinate and share information. Another interviewee said, "If we have unusual cases or adverse outcomes, then we have regular clinical meetings, look at the cases, pull them to pieces, and everybody tries to learn from those."

In addition, specialists communicated and reflected on the experimental methods they were conducting and developed a deeper understanding of one another's disciplines and how to fine-tune and combine their efforts to greater effect. As one doctor put it: "All these problematic cases add to our experience as doctors, it makes us talk to embryologists, to pharmacists; it matures us, it helps us understand things, the physiology of different races and diseases, how drugs work for them, what their medical predispositions are."

The good thing is, standard cases also benefit from that. Another doctor said, "The effort of treating difficult patients intensifies the interaction among our doctors, embryologists, and nurses. And we tend to take that with us, and to do it for the next patient who enters our office." Through practice and continual communication, clinics were able to fine-tune new ways of working.

Therefore, make sure to take on difficult cases that force different people in diverse disciplines to coordinate and work together. Organize meetings in which people reflect on their experiences trying to serve difficult clients or complete challenging projects, so everyone can derive knowledge and apply it on a wider scale.

Translation and Codification

There is a third and final necessary step to the learning cycle: after having reflected on the experiments conducted, you need to translate these insights into explicit if not tangible models, technologies, and procedures—a process generally referred to as knowledge codification.

More Than Just Talk

Based on their experiments, and their conversations with colleagues, doctors in IVF clinics develop and fine-tune treatment protocols, which they capture in explicit check-lists. The checklists force them to be precise, in terms of the exact implications for the treatment of patients. As one doctor put it: "It's hard, but treating severe cases comes with its rewards. I'm not talking only about the thrill of cracking a difficult case. I'm talking about the careful checklists that you put together and the resilience that you develop as you do that. Baby or no baby, the checklists and the ideas you tried stay with you."

I have to admit to being quite a fan of codification, in one way or another. Or perhaps a better way to put it is that I am not a fan (at all) of not engaging in codification, but just leaving things at "this was a good discussion." People often say, "This was a good experience; we have really learned from this." But without explicit output, I'm not so sure you have learned. I'm not sure you'll do better next time.

Codification, as a final stage after experimentation and reflection, forces people to be precise in terms of the consequences for subsequent actions. Without it, after a reflective meeting, people may often even think they've agreed on something, only to realize that, once they're codifying (e.g., putting it on paper) and translating it into explicit consequences for future behavior, they're not entirely sure precisely what they had agreed on. Codification is the litmus test. Translating what is learned is a necessary element of innovation.

Hence, you need to arrive at something quite tangible, something that you (quite literally) hold in your hand when you walk out of that meeting: your company's equivalent of a doctor's checklist and revised protocol. Perhaps for you it is a list of specifications, resource commitments, or even a prototype. But you need to have something, because without it, it's just talk.

In reality, the three stages of the learning cycle flow into one another. For example, people engage in reflective communication (stage two) while they are experimenting (i.e., stage one). Similarly, the topic of the reflection meeting (stage two) will often be the translation and codification of their experiences (i.e., stage three). But whether completely separate or not, all three behaviors are needed to arrive at innovation and to renew the ways your organization works, perhaps even continuously.

If you want to test how your team is doing, consider administering the short questionnaire shown in figure 9-1. The psychometric measures are all academically solid and carefully validated; a team member will take about five minutes to complete it. The measures capture to what extent the team engages in learning behavior.[2]

The question—raised at the beginning of this chapter—was, how do you stimulate people to engage in this type of learning behavior? What will it take to actually get them to do it? Because it's one thing to say what people's behavior should be, but usually quite another to actually get them to engage in it every day. My (quite simple) answer to this justified and relevant question is: Do difficult stuff.

I do not mean difficult stuff as in "Let's enter China" (for a Western company that has never operated abroad

FIGURE 9-1

Measuring the learning behavior of your team

	NEVER	RARELY SOMETIMES	OFTEN	ALWAYS
EXPERIMENTATION				
This team comes up with many new ideas about how work should be done.				
If a new way of doing work is introduced, it often comes from within the team.				
The team is frequently the source of ideas that are copied by other teams.				
Points per answer in this column	1	2	3	4	5
Subtotal				
TOTAL EXPERIMENTATION SCORE *(add the numbers in the subtotal row)*				
COMMUNICATION				
There is open communcation in this team.				
Everyone in this team has a chance to express their opinion.				
Team members maintain a high level of exchange.				
Points per answer in this column	1	2	3	4	5
Subtotal				
TOTAL COMMUNICATION SCORE *(add the numbers in the subtotal row)*				
CODIFICATION				
This team carefully documents how it does its work.				
This team has a formal system to capture its good ideas.				
This team attempts to record its best practices.				
Points per answer in this column	1	2	3	4	5
Subtotal				
TOTAL CODIFICATION SCORE *(add the numbers in the subtotal row)*				

RESULTS				
Multiply your total scores from each section	× Total Experimentation Score	× Total Communication Score	Total Codification Score	= **GRAND TOTAL**

If your team scores well below **700**, it's in trouble: It does not display sufficient learning behavior, and it may be employing bad practices.

before*) or "Let's develop a new product in a completely different line of business" or something as radical as that. I mean, let's make a challenging variant of our existing product or service. Let's make a version of our car that could drive from Paris to Dakar; let's treat that forty-nine-year-old lady with one ovary; let's develop a wound-care product for that (fortunately very rare but also) very stinky ailment; let's take on that difficult legal case that no one else wants to touch. It needs to be a challenge, but one related to what you're already doing, one from which you could see or at least feasibly suspect that its learnings will spill over into your normal-day stuff.

Then treat it as an innovation project: don't expect to make money on the action itself; organize get-togethers with the relevant actors to explicitly discuss the learnings from the experiment, and make sure to translate them into concrete follow-up procedures, technologies, or models. An organization that builds this into its system will be much less susceptible to developing bad practices,

---

* I once met an executive who told me his company entered China just because it was so difficult, the thinking being, "If we can make it there, we can make it anywhere." Perhaps not surprisingly, it was a disaster. I think such a huge step in terms of making your life difficult (like a car company not getting into rally racing but immediately into speedboat racing) might be too much of a good thing.

much less likely to stick with antiquated habits and routines when they are no longer ideal. Taking on challenging cases triggers renewal, innovation, and simply better ways of doing things.

Thus, "change for change's sake" (the previous chapter) is one way to organize for innovation; taking on challenging cases is another one. I have a third recommendation for how to organize for continual innovation: balance exploration with exploitation. We'll explore this through the example of Sadler's Wells Theatre in London. I think I've learned more from it, about organizing for continual innovation, than from any other organization.

CHAPTER 10

Balance Exploration with Exploitation

Exploration is essential for long-term innovation and renewal. IVF clinics explored difficult cases, the *Independent* explored a smaller-trim newspaper, Eden McCallum explored a freelance structure for its consulting firm, and so on. These organizations freed themselves of the status quo, tried new things, and succeeded at creating new opportunities that otherwise wouldn't have been possible. But you can't spend all of your time and energy

with exploration. You also need to focus on exploiting—
and profiting—from an existing competitive advantage.

The challenge is that exploration and exploitation
(borrowing terminology first used by the famous Stanford
University professor James March) require organizations
to balance freedom and long-term innovation, both of
which are requirements for exploration, with the stabil-
ity and hierarchy that are needed for exploitation.[1] This
is extremely difficult, and pretty much every CEO I have
ever interviewed has mentioned the challenge of achieving
this balance (although perhaps not necessarily using these
exact terms).

Some organizations manage to achieve balance, however, and one of the best, in my humble opinion, is Sadler's
Wells, a centuries-old theater in London, which I've extensively studied and visited on numerous occasions.

The Center of Innovation

When Alistair Spalding took over as CEO in 2004, Sadler's
Wells Theatre was in turmoil. Although the previous CEO,
Jean-Luc Choplin, a former managing director of the Paris
Opera Ballet who also helped launch Disneyland Paris, had

a wealth of experience, a bold vision, and daring ideas, the theater struggled under his tutelage. The shows he promoted were extravagantly expensive, came in over budget or were canceled, and attendance figures disappointed, while box-office personnel went on strike and four female executives launched sexual discrimination cases against him.

Spalding shared the theater board's ambition to play an active role in developing the performing arts. He also realized the company needed a clear and consistent direction, one that people could understand and rally behind. Therefore, he proclaimed a new vision and ambition for the company: "to be the centre of innovation in dance."

He knew he had his work cut out for him. "I was very excited at the opportunity before me," he told me. "But I also distinctly remember an uneasy feeling . . . To tell you the truth, I wasn't exactly sure at the time precisely how I would manage the balancing act of playing it safe—housing shows that did not involve heavy investment and would likely have robust advance ticket sales— while investing in the co-production of untried innovative productions."

As we'll see, Spalding managed to find the right balance between exploration and exploitation. But, first, let's look at the exploration side of his strategy.

Spalding and his team didn't create new products or enter new markets in order to set up the organization for continual innovation. Instead, they followed an "open focus" strategy. They chose to focus exclusively on contemporary dance, but at the same time, they opened themselves up to outsiders and established alliances, both of which provided the knowledge, ideas, and talent necessary to foster new ideas.

That's the idea of open focus. Rather than jump into new fields in order to innovate, you renew and reinvigorate existing businesses, and look for inspiration and knowledge from outside sources.

Narrowing the Focus

Three theaters—the main stage with 1,500 seats, the adjoining Lilian Baylis Studio with 180 seats, and The Peacock Theatre with 1,000 seats—would exclusively focus on contemporary dance. This choice was fairly audacious since contemporary dance is generally regarded as a niche genre. But it wasn't crazy. The main stage had been designed for dance, and in the past, before Choplin's short reign, Sadler's Wells had gained a reputation—especially among artists—of being the premier house for contemporary dance in all of Europe. So it made sense to double-down on contemporary dance.

Given their narrow focus, however, Spalding and his team knew that they had to offer diverse programs. Kingsley Jayasekera, director of marketing and communications at the time, explained it: "The old idea among theaters was if you want to do dance, you have to diversify into other forms of theater. What we did was diversify within the art form; we offer flamenco or tango, we do hip-hop. We also have drumming performances, opera, ballet, a circus-based performance, but it's all dance-led." Spalding and his team believed that their exclusive focus on contemporary dance would eventually enable the theater to be a tastemaker and catalyst for the art form.

Developing a Platform Strategy

In order to offer diverse programming, the Sadler's Wells team turned the theater into a platform of sorts. Platform strategies have become all the rage in recent years, in the wake of the success of the likes of Apple, Facebook, Twitter, YouTube, and other technology companies. As you may know, a platform strategy implies that the firm provides a platform, while external parties largely produce the content—apps, personal posts, or video clips—that attracts customers.

Sadler's Wells literally provides the stage for others to perform on, but has no dancers, orchestra, or choreographers of its own on the payroll. All performers are external to the company. They produce the content; Sadler's Wells provides the platform.

Ordinarily, this strategy would have been very risky. But running Sadler's like a platform allowed Spalding to attract a wide range of talented artists. Instead of being beholden to its own choreographers and dancers, who would have specific skills and concentrations, outside performers offered more reach and flexibility to Spalding and his programmers.

Of course, this meant that the Sadler's Wells team had to attract top talent. But it was confident that the sheer size of the theater would be a competitive advantage. Other theaters may have been willing to pay the same artists to come and perform on their stage too, but because Sadler's Wells is so large—bigger than any other theater suitable for dance—its programmers were often able to pay them a bit more since it could sell more tickets.

In addition—and, perhaps, most important, as a competitive advantage in securing performers—the scale of

Sadler's Wells was attractive to artists for other reasons: artists and dance companies care about their own brand name, and performing at Sadler's Wells simply leads to more exposure than performing at other theaters. Performing at Sadler's Wells is a prestigious accomplishment, due to its size. As Farooq Chaudhuri—producer of the innovative and successful Akram Khan Company—told me, "When we started, we said to each other, 'I hope, one day, we will be performing at Sadler's Wells.'"

To further lure talent, the Sadler's Wells team also organized courses for making work specifically for a large stage, and they hired an experienced, internal producer (Emma Gladstone, herself a former dancer) to assist and advise external dance companies in developing its product.

Creating Alliances

The Sadler's Wells team also created an associate artists program. Spalding approached a number of highly visible, rising stars in the field of contemporary dance and asked them to become formally affiliated with the theater. He offered associate artists free office space, access to the theater's practice studios, and if they wished, regular advice from Spalding and the in-house producer on the new shows they were working on. In return, Spalding asked them to premiere their new shows at Sadler's Wells Theatre.

Most artists eagerly agreed, and over the years, their number grew to sixteen. The benefits were clear; the association enabled both the artists and Sadler's Wells to enhance their pivotal resource: reputation. Artists gained a prestigious title and affiliation, but the reputation of Sadler's Wells also benefited. To have the dance world's hottest stars formally associated with the theater was prestigious and eye-catching. It attracted publicity, too. Each time one of the stars had a new show, it would premiere at Sadler's Wells, and the press would visit and write about it. In turn, the platform became even more attractive to other artists and content developers.

Spalding had another purpose in mind, though, with the associate artists program. He wanted the company to be a hub for dancers and artists. To accomplish this, he needed to bring them to the theater even when they weren't performing a show.

Each time I personally visited Sadler's Wells Theatre to interview people, I would see artists chatting in the cafeteria or corridor, looking at staging plans, or explaining to each other their ideas for a new show. These chance meetings, Spalding reasoned, would foster collaboration and innovation.

A Cultural Dating Agency

Spalding and his team didn't stop there, however. As believers in the idea that innovation often takes place at the boundaries of different (sub)fields, they started a research program, led by in-house producer Emma Gladstone, that sought to foster collaborations between dancers, artists, painters, musicians, set designers, and the like.

In a sense, Sadler's became what they jokingly called a cultural dating agency.

Scouting

The first step they took was to start a process of continual scouting for external content that in their case—contemporary dance—meant visiting hundreds of shows of artists, in fringe theaters, theater schools, foreign dance companies, and so on. Gladstone told me, "I see about two hundred shows per year." Sadler's Wells is explicitly and continuously on the lookout for new artists, for people who can potentially cooperate to make work for its stage.

Scouting is not unique to the world of the performing arts. Felipe Monteiro—now a professor at INSEAD—did his PhD research at London Business School on British Telecom's (BT) external scouting units that set up in Silicon Valley and other tech hubs. The units, which were staffed with senior executives, sought to discover external technologies that might be attractive and relevant for BT. Scouting allowed BT to tap into a wider range of innovation than was possible inside its own headquarters and also improved its decision making. Instead of judging the merits of an idea on paper, it could see a prototype in action.

Sadler's Wells is no different from BT. By scouting, it increased the scale of its talent and innovation, and could see how ideas may or may not work in live settings.

Make People Meet

After finding new talent, the team would invite them to dinner. Yes, seriously. Gladstone organized something she called "Dinner Dance." The team regularly invited a relatively small group of people—artists, choreographers, some producers—from the field of dance but also from adjacent fields (e.g., filmmaking, puppetry, lighting) to come for a meal. Other than the menu, there was no agenda, no obligations; the point was just to eat and drink, be merry, and get to know one another.

Of course, Gladstone didn't just invite a random bunch of people; she thought carefully about interesting combinations of individuals (and, hence, potential collaborations), and she would also deliberately sit certain people next to one another at the table. But the general idea was to bring artists into contact with one another in an informal way. If the artists hit it off, if they liked each other and each other's work and ideas, a collaborative project might ensue, and the cultural dating agency would have done its job.

Again, the idea of informal meetings has its equivalent in the business world. A former colleague at London Business School, Bjorn Lovas (who unfortunately died in a mountaineering accident some years ago), studied the innovative Danish hearing-aid company Oticon—nicknamed The Spaghetti Company.* He told me that

---

* So-called because there is no simple formal organizational structure; all people are connected to other employees in the firm through a range of different formal and informal relationships, without any formal hierarchy.

its new head office included wider staircases than the architect had originally envisioned, so that when people met on the stairs, they could stop and chat, without having to make way for people behind them. Similarly, when Steve Jobs designed Pixar's new head office, he deliberately created a layout where employees would automatically have many informal, chance meetings with colleagues from all over the firm. Therefore, he wanted one cafeteria for the whole company, common coffee corners (instead of people having their own machine in their unit) and, famously, only one restroom for the entire twelve-hundred-person company (although his fellow board members, weary of bladder problems, convinced him to have one on each floor).

Whether you make people meet for dinner, on a staircase, or in the restroom, the idea is that regular informal, chance meetings create a breeding ground for collaborations, which are an important prerequisite for innovation to occur.

Muck About in the Lab

The next step in Sadler's Wells's cultural dating agency was to give people a chance to experiment. In order to do so, it offered studio time for artists who wanted to work on a new idea. Sometimes, it even went as far as to put them on the payroll for a week or two. It gave young and promising yet cash-strapped artists an opportunity to explore new ideas. This free time, used to muck about and just try things out, was another crucial step in the innovation process.

Mucking about as a habit—trying out crazy things with playfulness—is an essential component of an organization fit for continual innovation. Sometimes it doesn't work at all (but then there's not much harm done), but sometimes it does. When the team at Sadler's Wells likes what an artist is doing in the studio, it may ask them to develop their ideas into an actual show.

Suck It and See

If possible, Sadler's Wells will first schedule a new show for a short period at its smallest venue, the Lilian Baylis Studio, which seats 180. Or, for a big production, it'll schedule it on the main stage for only a few days or so. Artists can then test their ideas, and the risk for Sadler's Wells is lowered because it sees the show in action. If the show doesn't quite work, the team may scrap it or make adaptations. If and when the show does work—in the view of the team members and also the initial audience and the art critics—Sadler's Wells will bring it back the next season and put it on the main stage for an entire week or longer.

This strategy, too, isn't unique to the arts. Stanford University professor Kathleen Eisenhardt and her coauthor Shona Brown conducted a well-known study in the 1990s comparing several dozen firms in fast-moving businesses—mostly tech companies from Silicon Valley, but also some from Seattle (such as Dell), and some fast-moving consumer companies (such as Gillette)—making pair-wise comparisons between successful firms and their similar but less successful competitors. One of the things they found was that the more successful firms relied more on experimental products: rather than widely launching a new product or service, they tested it in a corner of the market. If it was successful—sometimes after changes—they would proceed with a marketwide launch. If it wasn't successful, they'd forget the whole thing altogether.

Many industries find it very hard to forecast how the market will react to a new product or service, precisely because it is new. The best way to get reliable information is to test it on a small scale. Or, to use a unique British expression: suck it and see. If it has never been tried before, the only way to find out if it works, is to just try it out.

A Striking Balance

As I mentioned at the top of this chapter, exploration needs to be counterbalanced with exploitation. To Sadler's Wells's credit, it managed to do so by following a three-pronged approach: it created a clear structural separation between its exploration and exploitation efforts, it concentrated exclusively on each for a set period of time, and it made achieving balance a constant point of conversation.

Structural Separation

In order to achieve balance, Sadler's Wells engages in structural separation. The main stage and the small Lilian Baylis Studio are pegged for exploration, and the third stage, The Peacock Theatre, which seats about a thousand, is best fit for exploitation. Or, as Spalding put it, "[The Peacock] is there for only one reason: to make money—that's its raison d'être."

This type of separation, which is common, can pose problems. Usually, organizations create one subunit that does the innovative, exploratory stuff, while another division takes care of exploitation by making a profit from existing products. Often the two organizational units are housed in separate buildings and locations. The problem with this method is that the firm hardly ever manages to exploit its explorations. A famous example is the old Xerox lab (later renamed PARC). Its explorers invented the graphical user interface, the laser printer, and Ethernet technology, but its exploitation unit never commercialized them.

To prevent disjointedness, Sadler's Wells decided that one management team would oversee its exploitation and exploration activities. There is no separate program for The Peacock, for example, not even a separate website. Sadler's Wells organizes the two parts—its exploration and exploitation units—as one coherent organization.

Flipping Back and Forth

Sadler's Wells also concentrates on exploitation for a specific period of time and then shifts its focus to exploration. This isn't as odd as it seems, as Cisco and Hewlett-Packard do similar things.[2]

Sadler's Wells flips back and forth twice each year. In the summer, its management team schedules tried-and-tested shows that will sell out and generate a healthy profit. After the summer, it offers much riskier, innovative stuff. Then, around Christmas, it again schedules shows it knows will sell out. Blockbuster productions such as Matthew Bourne's reinterpretation of *Swan Lake* can bring in up to 80 percent of the year's profits from 40 percent of the year's revenue. Or, as managing director Chrissy Sharp elegantly summarized it: "You can't fuck up Christmas." Then it's back to exploration.

Like structural separation, flipping back and forth can be problematic. If treated in an ad hoc manner, flipping can be very disruptive to the organization, if not paralyze it entirely.

Sadler's Wells, however, avoids disruption because its flipping is well planned and routine. It doesn't debate on whether and when to flip, and it doesn't make hurried or crisis-driven decisions about changes. Each year, the theater's flipping follows a stable and predictable rhythm (just like the seasons in nature). It's this predictability—well known to the entire organization—that makes it easy to manage.

Constant Balancing

Last, the management team makes sure that the balance between innovative shows and money makers remains a constant topic of conversation. These conversations tend to take place in front of a whiteboard in the corridor next to Spalding's office, which displays the draft schedule for the next year: "Are we getting the balance right? Do we need a few more safe shows? Or is it a bit too mainstream, and do we need a few more experimental things?" The schedule represents the balance between exploitation and exploration products, and these conversations occur all the time.

Organizations usually either go all-in with exploitation, focusing on short-term profitability, or exploration, losing themselves by jumping into new opportunities all the time. However, the constant attention the Sadler's Wells team pays to balance prevents it from falling into this trap.

Figure 10-1 displays the three options companies can pursue to create a balance between exploitation and exploration activities. These different options serve the

FIGURE 10-1

Three options for balancing exploitation and exploration

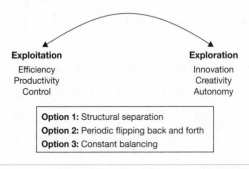

Exploitation
Efficiency
Productivity
Control

Exploration
Innovation
Creativity
Autonomy

Option 1: Structural separation
Option 2: Periodic flipping back and forth
Option 3: Constant balancing

same purpose but each has particular advantages and disadvantages, as discussed above. The options aren't mutually exclusive—companies can use one of them or, as Sadler's Wells did, pursue them in combination.

Means and Ends Semantics

When I interview a top manager about his or her company's exploration efforts, I always make it a point to ask, "Why do you do this innovation stuff?" Invariably, the answer is something along the lines of "Well, we need to innovate to make sure we have something to exploit and profit from in the future." And they are right.

But when I posed the same question to Spalding and Sharp, they were completely silent. For a moment I feared that the question had offended them. Finally, Sharp chimed in with an answer: "Because . . . that's what we do: innovation."

Then I understood. Sadler's Wells doesn't explore new artistic avenues in order to have something to exploit in the future; instead, it engages in profit-seeking exploitation so it can explore new things. Exploration is the end; exploitation is the means.

Of course, what is the end and what is the means is just a matter of semantics; eventually you need to do a bit of both, regardless of which comes first. However, semantics matter; it matters for the culture of a place and for its identity. Sadler's Wells's identity revolves around innovation; it's what Sadler's Wells is about, and everybody knows this.

When I talk to people about their work, invariably what excites them is not their companies' wonderful earnings per share or return on assets. What they love talking about is the great new things their companies are doing: their new products, and their new technologies, approaches, and business models. I wonder whether more companies would be better off with an innovation-first culture and identity, like Sadler's Wells's, where profit provides the necessary means to innovate and create exciting new things in the future.

Diagnostic and Intervention

Sadler's Wells's success as a nonprofit arts organization is applicable to businesses of all sorts. Of course, a theater company is different from a for-profit business, but so are all other organizations and organizational forms. Each is unique. Yet, all also share important aspects, regardless of their sector and governance model, whether they're a listed company, a family firm, an arts organization, or a partnership. Those similarities are what we are after. I suggest that you consider our visit to Sadler's Wells as our own external scouting.

All organizations need to choose where they want to be on the scale between exploration and exploitation, and then act accordingly. The little questionnaire in figure 10-2 is a simple diagnostic tool that will help you determine where your organization currently is on the curve between exploitation and exploration.

FIGURE 10-2

The exploitation-exploration framework

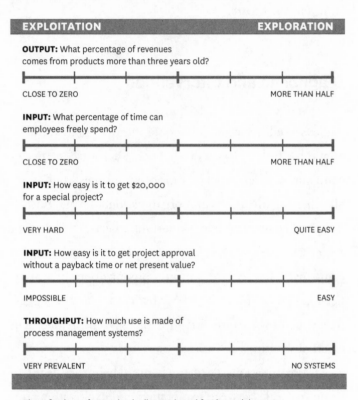

EXPLOITATION   **EXPLORATION**

OUTPUT: What percentage of revenues
comes from products more than three years old?

CLOSE TO ZERO   MORE THAN HALF

INPUT: What percentage of time can
employees freely spend?

CLOSE TO ZERO   MORE THAN HALF

INPUT: How easy is it to get $20,000
for a special project?

VERY HARD   QUITE EASY

INPUT: How easy is it to get project approval
without a payback time or net present value?

IMPOSSIBLE   EASY

THROUGHPUT: How much use is made of
process management systems?

VERY PREVALENT   NO SYSTEMS

These five items form a simple diagnostic tool for determining your
organization's position on the exploitation-exploration curve.
To use this diagnostic, mark approximately where your firm falls on
each slider.

If your marks fall mostly to the **LEFT SIDE**, your firm is showing
characteristics of an **EXPLOITATION** orientation.

If your marks fall mostly to the **RIGHT SIDE**, your firm is more oriented
toward **EXPLORATION**.

Question One

The first question concerns what percentage of your company's revenues is from products fewer than three years old. (If your industry is particularly fast- or slow-moving, use a number of years that is appropriate for you.) If your company very much depends on long-established products, it is clearly on the exploitation side. That is not necessarily bad, but if you've declared that innovation is paramount to your strategy and you score much on the left side of this question, there's a problem—or at least a misfit. In that case, you need to change something.

The tool can also be considered a guideline for intervention. If your stated strategy is about exploration, but you score toward exploitation on this question, this should prompt you to increase your investment in innovation. Consider, for example, the highly successful 3M Corporation, a very innovative company that has been around for a long time. It's also very profitable, with an average return on assets of 29 percent and gross margins topping 50 percent over the past two decades. It famously employs a so-called 30 percent rule: at least 30 percent of each division's revenues have to come from products less than four years old. If this target is not achieved, 3M automatically increases its investment in innovation (even if the net present value of a similar investment in existing products is higher).

Hence, this criterion represents an output rule. Of course, you can debate and fudge a bit what is really a "new product" and is not, but the principle is clear: hitting the number is a prerequisite, so set yourself a target in accordance with your stated strategy and stick to it.

Question Two

The second question concerns what percentage of their time employees can spend freely, for instance, pursuing a pet project they believe in but that is not part of their formal task description. This is an input to innovation (in contrast to the previous output-driven rule). If your company is about innovation—or so you say—you need to give people time to experiment and muck about. I'm not saying that every organization needs to do this, but if you want to be innovative, there's no substitute for it.

This input rule can be more or less formalized. Google, for example, famously formalized it in its 20 percent rule. Every employee has to spend 20 percent of their time on things that are not in their task description, and they will be judged on that.* 3M has a similar rule. Hence, it's not the case that this is the percentage of time in which you are allowed to do nothing, file your nails, watch television, or browse your Facebook pages. In your annual review, for instance, you will be asked, "What did you do and achieve in that 20 percent?" Yet, it is 20 percent without boundaries and without an assignment and target. It's time to muck about.

Question Three

The third item—also an input rule—concerns a question that Gary Hamel, visiting professor at London Business School, tends to ask when and wherever you run into him. Bump into him in the corridor, the cafeteria, or the men's room and he will poke his finger into your chest, peer at you through his slightly stern glasses, and say, "How easy is it in your firm to get a $20,000 budget approved?"

It's a good question (although perhaps not in the men's room), because what he really means is that if

---

* Although, admittedly, I did hear a Google executive jokingly say, "That 20 percent? It's the weekend."

you want to pursue an idea, a hunch about something new, and just need a very modest budget of a mere 20K, can you get it quite easily in your firm? Or even for such a small amount of money, would you need to jump through all sorts of administrative hoops, spreadsheets, and rounds of approval? If you're a thrifty company focused on exploitation, there's not much wrong with answering "very hard" to this perusing question; but if you're a firm said to be determined to innovate, you need to make such modest funds easily available to enable your employees to pursue an innovative idea—just as Sadler's Wells gives modest budgets to its artists to muck about. Without easy access to such modest funds, you will stifle innovation.

Question Four

The fourth item on the questionnaire concerns another input measure: How easy is it in your firm to get project approval without numbers, such as a payback time or net present value calculation? Rest assured, I have nothing against numbers. I love numbers; my own academic research, for instance, is highly quantitative. However, numbers can also be a dud, because they focus us on what we can measure, at the expense of things we can't quantify.

Truly new things are often all but impossible to quantify. How do you estimate the market for mobile phones when they don't yet exist? Market research apparently said very categorically, "There is no market for a mobile telephone." Insist on hard numbers from the outset of an idea and all you will get are incremental ideas. If you say your organization is about true innovation and about developing things and markets that do not yet exist, you cannot insist on numbers at an early stage. Like Sadler's Wells, initially, you will have to rely on a hunch, an idea, and perhaps the enthusiasm and belief of your people. Only later on, when investment requirements increase as well, can you start to insist on numbers.

If your organization is about exploitation, fine; insist on all the numbers you can think of immediately. But if you want to produce something new, you will have to be a bit more patient.

Question Five

The final question is more of a throughput item and also requires a bit of explanation. Recall the research on ISO 9000 and other process management systems by professors Mary Benner and Michael Tushman that I discussed in chapter 2? They showed that companies that rely heavily on such systems see their innovation plummet in the long run. These systems are wonderful for efficiency and exploitation, but not so much for exploration.

Again, if your stated strategy is about carefully strengthening and exploiting an existing competitive advantage, by all means implement a careful process management system. But if a firm states that it wants to be an innovator and a developer of truly new products and markets, but its internal organization is lined with process management, standardizing procedures, best practices, and reducing margins for errors, that's a misfit.

―――――――――

These five items form a simple diagnostic tool for determining your internal organization's position on the exploitation-exploration curve. It's also an intervention tool in the sense that it defines levers you can pull to change your firm's position on the curve and find your desired balance.

―――――――――

In the next chapter, I return briefly to the example of Sadler's Wells for the fourth and final principle for organizing for continual innovation: Be varied and selective. Be an avid gardener and let a thousand flowers blossom (after the ancient Chinese proverb), but also subsequently annihilate 999 of them ruthlessly and systematically.

CHAPTER 11

Be Varied and Selective

To create different ways of doing things, your firm needs variation, in terms of different processes, people, ideas, technologies, and so on. As the famous Austrian economist Joseph Schumpeter, beginning in the 1930s, argued on the topic of innovation and entrepreneurship, creating different ways of doing things rests on your ability to develop new combinations of resources.

There is a lot of advice on how to increase variation, and lots of firms follow it: promote pluralism and diversity, let people think outside the box, generate ideas, and so on. In other words, let a thousand flowers bloom.

However, that is only half the story. You also need to be selective. In other words, you need to let 999 of those flowers die, which is something a lot of companies struggle with.

Let's tackle variation, first.

Variation

Like Sadler's Wells Theatre, companies over the past decade have become well aware that if they want innovation and constant renewal, they will need to foster some form of variation within their firms. There are myriad ways to do this, but open innovation and what I call "hybrid vigor" are two of the most promising.

Open Innovation

As you may know, open innovation is the idea that innovation shouldn't take place in a carefully guarded, separate building with extra security measures and access control (to keep ideas in and snooping outsiders out) but, instead, should involve different parties from outside the firm. This is why companies experiment with all sorts of online idea-generation schemes and external scouting units (such as BT's unit in Silicon Valley that is there to spot new technologies). Open innovation can also take the form of cooperating with competitors; consulting with firms from other lines of business with different capabilities and skills; or inviting ideas from customers, suppliers, and anyone else who is not inbred and has a fresh point of view.

A heralded example of open innovation is LEGO, which underwent a rather dramatic turnaround over the last decade. It went from pending bankruptcy in 2003—suffering a $235 million loss—to overtaking Barbie maker Mattel as the largest toy company in the world in 2014, having quadrupled its revenues in the decade between. Although there are undoubtedly various causes for this revival, the company itself accords much of its turnaround success to its renewed approach to open innovation. For example, LEGO nowadays actively invites and engages users to submit new product designs, which are then tested out for sale on its website, after which the most successful ones find their way into retail. It doesn't just invent and develop its own new product designs; it lets its wide base of customers do that work.

I also saw this in action at the British model train-maker Hornby in a situation similar to LEGO's. Hornby's CEO Frank Martin turned the company around after a near-bankruptcy, quintupling its share price in five years.* Martin changed the company's strategy to target adult collectors and hobbyists, giving a prominent role to product innovation. In the process, Hornby opened up its innovation model; Martin set up alliances with digital electronics and software companies, figuring that a recombination of their different skills and capabilities should be able to lead to innovation, and it did. Furthermore, he set up collectors' clubs and online communities, and hired personnel specifically employed to maintain and scan these communities for new product ideas. The technology for Hornby's innovative steam engine, for example, originally came from a user rather than from its own R&D department.

Hybrid Vigor

Organizations can also enhance variation though acquisition. By infusing itself with new resources and combining them with its preexisting resources, an organization can create new ways of doing things and enhance itself through hybrid vigor, a term I've borrowed from biology.

---

* Although, in recent years, it's gotten in trouble again, I believe by trying to grow and diversify too fast.

Hybrid vigor refers to a small infusion of external DNA that can quite quickly revitalize an entire inbred population. There is research in biology on hybrid vigor (also known as heterosis) in glamorous populations such as corn, but there is also some evidence of the process occurring in livestock and even humans.[1]

In management, hybrid vigor would occur through an infusion of external organizational DNA—in the form of processes, people, ideas, and technologies—for example, through the takeover and integration of another firm. In that sense, organizational hybrid vigor (or social heterosis) could potentially provide the same effect and hence be a substitute for the mechanism of "change for change's sake," as I discussed earlier. Arguably, acquisitions provide disruption to the present-day workings of an organization—as does change for change's sake—but, as argued earlier too, not all disruption is always bad. In fact, perhaps it is a necessary condition for (process) innovation to occur in the first place.

As a case in point, a research assistant and I interviewed executives in the pharmaceutical company Pfizer, which had recently acquired Warner-Lambert, a conglomerate that included the pharmaceutical division Parke-Davis.[2] Pfizer had wanted to gain full control over the anticholesterol drug Lipitor,

213

which it had been co-promoting with Parke-Davis; integrate Parke-Davis into Pfizer's organization; and sell off the rest of Warner-Lambert. The executives told us, however, that during the integration process, they saw that many of Parke-Davis's functions were organized differently from their own. In response, management decided not to impose Pfizer's processes on the newly acquired business but rather allow managers to develop entirely new ways of doing things.

This decision generated some integration troubles. There were reports of power struggles, culture clashes, and people trying to maintain the status quo. But gradually, new organizational practices began to emerge. For example, Pfizer developed new approaches to human resources ("Our people-management processes are better now; we learned the softer things like talent management"), to resource management ("Before, we were so used to having so much money that we didn't think about efficient use of resources"), and to decision making ("There is now a more open culture, a faster decision-making process").

Pfizer had originally bought Parke-Davis just to gain full control of the drug Lipitor, but while integrating the company and seeing how differently it operated, management began to realize that the Pfizer organization had become rigid and complacent. As one manager put it, "We were so successful, which had led to an insular, comfortable state of mind. This acquisition was a consciousness-raising exercise. It made us realize that we could do better; now we realize there are other ways of doing things." Thus, an acquisition can make people aware that there are different ways of doing things and that it may be time to consider a change. In Pfizer—similar to the effects of change for change's sake described in chapter 8—the infusion of new practices from Parke-Davis led to a revitalization within various parts of its organization that were at risk of becoming rigid.

Selection

Many organizations make some sort of arrangements to try and stimulate variation. They have some idea-generation scheme, an online notice board through which employees can submit proposals or even a competition with bonuses and awards. They then form a committee or small group of middle managers who first sift through the proposals. Their task is to select the most promising ideas and forward them to top management. Invariably, these middle managers have their own biases and beliefs, and those greatly influence their selections. One such bias is that they are much more afraid of making so-called type I errors (false positives) than of making type II errors (false negatives).

These middle managers will not necessarily forward the best ideas to their bosses, and probably not even the ideas they think are best. They'll forward the ideas they think their bosses will like and want to see. What they hate and really want to avoid is forwarding an idea about which their boss will say, "Why did you forward that?!" Because that will make them look—and feel—stupid. It's bad for their reputations.

What they mind a lot less is type II errors: the false negative of not forwarding something—and hence killing it off—that, in fact, their boss would have liked. No one will ever know about that one. The error will likely go unnoticed.

As a consequence, these various forms of idea-generation schemes seldom become a real success, not because they do not create variation—they do—but because they fail at selection. They fail at selection because middle managers make biased and conservative decisions, and subsequently, top managers also bring in their biased beliefs and choices. Properly organizing for selection is where most progress can be made when it comes to organizing for innovation: you need to become better at letting 999 flowers die.

Let Selection Happen

Just as you need to organize variation, you need to set up a process that systematically manages selection. The first principle to be aware of in designing such a system is that top managers do not make the selection themselves; instead, they need to organize for it to happen.

A good example can be found at the large British television production company FremantleMedia. Tony Cohen—its previous CEO—would be confronted with many proposals for new television productions. However, he resisted the temptation to select the ones he himself considered most promising. Instead, he built an internal system that would identify the most promising ideas for him.

For example, every year, the company organized an event, the Fremantle Market, where senior executives from Fremantle's various production companies would present their ideas for new television shows to one another (usually in the form of a trial episode). Since Cohen had set up an internal licensing system, ideas for new productions that would attract the interest of others within the company would automatically be funded; if there was a lack of interest, the proposal would fail to acquire the financial resources necessary for it to be developed further; hence it would die an early death.

This is the idea of enabling selection to happen. Rather than senior executives making the choices themselves, they implement processes that lead to selection among the alternatives. In this way, the organization avoids being overly reliant on the preferences and biases of any one individual.

Tap into the Wisdom of Your Crowd

The example of FremantleMedia also highlights a second principle of selection: that it uses and relies on the collective wisdom of the people working within the organization. Cohen told me, "I don't do the selection [of new television productions]; why would I know better than anyone else in the company? That is not my responsibility. It is my responsibility to organize for it to happen." He had designed a process to systematically tap into the insights of Fremantle's internal crowd.

Another good example is Intel, in the days when it still relied heavily on the production of DRAM memory chips. As Stanford University professor Robert Burgelman carefully documented, Intel allowed engineers to work on what they called embryonic technologies: new, early-stage variants of semiconductors.[3] For such new, innovative products, it is impossible to compute any reliable numbers (in terms of market size, demand growth, margin, or a variant of a net present value calculation), simply because the products and markets do not yet exist.

But Intel had decentralized its organization, giving its highly skilled engineers local R&D budgets and ample autonomy to decide for themselves what they were going to work on. When top managers observed more and more of their own engineers abandoning projects centered on the old DRAMs, gradually flocking toward a new technology called microprocessors, they realized it was time to change their strategy. They abandoned DRAMs and began to focus on microprocessors, a central product in the rapidly evolving computer industry.

Andy Grove—then Intel's CEO—said, "It looks like a Darwinian process: we let the best ideas win . . . You dance around it a bit, until a wider and wider group in the company becomes clear about it."[4] As a CEO, he followed the decisions his collective employees were making.

219

In the absence of reliable numbers, you have to rely on something else. Relying on the opinion of an individual top manager is risky, because any individual is likely to get it wrong and to be biased by emotions and past allegiances. However, combining the collective insights of a large group of skilled employees can circumvent this problem and enable a manager to tap into the knowledge of the crowd. Importantly, these middle managers—both in FremantleMedia and in Intel—do not just collectively make the selection. They put their own resources on the line. Their individual budgets, time, and P&Ls represent their level of belief and commitment in the chosen option. Designing such a systematic way to capture the crowd's wisdom and commitment is a key element of optimizing a selection process.

Objectivize the Process

When it comes to selection, there will be winners and losers. Some people and products will receive resources—such as funding, staffing, and attention—but others will lose out. Making the selection objective and deliberately detaching it from personal opinions is important. Various research and case examples have confirmed the risk of "escalation of commitment" in selection processes: decision makers who hold on to a failing course of action for too long because it provided success in the past or because someone's reputation is tied to it.[5] Therefore, companies have to deliberately objectivize the process and decouple it from individual decision makers.

Intel provides another case in point: when it was producing both DRAMs and microprocessors, it let these products compete for scarce production capacity on its manufacturing line. Top management had designed a formula—called the production capacity allocation rule—that, using a variety of input numbers (such as efficiency, demand growth, and margins), would compute which product would get how much production capacity. The engineers in charge of production would then simply follow the formula given to them.

Importantly, this made the process objective. The formula was put together at a time when the discussion was still abstract and detached from any real products and concrete preferences. Once push came to shove, and decisions needed to be made about winners and losers, the organization just followed the formula it had constructed earlier.

By making such a process objective, the organization can limit political infighting and escalation of commitment.

It detaches the decision from individual interests and emotions, which allows new ideas to be selected and prosper. This made Intel—based on its move into microprocessors—one of the most successful companies the world of business has ever witnessed.

Let the Evidence Match the Investment

A fourth design principle for creating a successful selection system is to prevent it from being a one- or two-step process, and to build in a multitude of selection moments during which variation is gradually reduced while quantifiable information increases.

Consider Sadler's Wells Theatre. Table 11-1 summarizes the variation and selection system it designed. Recall that it starts out scouting a large variety of dancers whose work might be suitable for its theaters. It then invites a limited number of these artists to develop ideas, in an informal way, for potential new productions. Some artists come up with a concrete and innovative idea; if so, Sadler's Wells will make available studio time and a small budget for them to try out their ideas. If indeed the idea seems to be going somewhere, it increases investment to develop the idea into a show, which, if possible, will premiere in the group's

TABLE 11-1

How Sadler's Wells Theatre organizes for continual innovation

Sadler's Wells selection funnel	Costs	Resulting evidence	Number
Continuous external scouting for something or someone who might work at Sadler's Wells	Very low	Sadler's Wells sees the person and a show in action, but just as a hunch	Several hundred per year
Sadler's Wells invites promising artists to dinners and courses, putting a variety of people in touch with each other	Low	People develop and describe a concrete idea for a show	About one hundred artists
Artists who have come up with an innovative idea get studio time and a small budget, and are sometimes put on the payroll for a few weeks	Medium	The theater's executives and producers can see a rough prototype of the show in action	Two dozen
The show is scheduled in the smallest theater (a few hundred seats) or in the main theater (1,900 seats) for a few days	Substantial	Sales, customer feedback, newspaper reviews	Five
If successful, the show is scheduled in the main theater for several weeks	Very high	Sales and presales	Three

smallest theater. If the show becomes a box-office success, Sadler's Wells will schedule it again later for a longer period in its main theater.

This system works so well because it combines a number of complementary elements: there is not one selection step for new productions but a number of them. Moreover, with each step, variation is reduced, but investment increases. The example of Sadler's Wells shows that it is important to have many selection moments, rather than just one or two (as most companies do with their team of middle managers and top managers as the final selectors).

Moreover, the amount of hard information that the theater has about the proposed show increases as time goes on. Initially, the theater's producers begin with a hunch about particular artists. Then they ask these artists to develop an actual idea for a performance, which gives management something concrete to talk about. Some of these ideas will then be forwarded for trials in the theater's studio. Now, theater management can see part of a prototype show in action, and that means that it can already assess the concrete contours of the product. Once the show has been finalized and scheduled in the small theater, there are box-office figures and critics' reviews to look at, which means the evidence has become very hard indeed. Hence, investment may increase with each selection step, but so does the evidence available. That is also a crucial, general design element: let the evidence match the investment.

We can see the same characteristics in Intel's innovation system: initially, the company based its embryonic technologies on very little data, just a hunch by an engineer, but concurrently the required investment was small. By the time the technologies reached the stage of production—which required a significant investment—only a small proportion of the initial embryonic ideas were left. Yet, for these, Intel had ample hard numbers that it could use as input for its production capacity allocation rule, which would cull the selection of the remaining technologies even further.

Companies that successfully manage the selection of their innovation systems incorporate a multitude of selection steps. At each step, both investment and information go up, while the variety of initiatives is reduced.

Give People a Box for Channeling Creativity

"Successful firms are characterized by maintaining bottom-up driven internal experimentation and selection processes while simultaneously maintaining top driven strategic intent," Burgelman wrote.[6] What he meant is that firms need to organize for bottom-up initiatives through variation and selection, as described earlier in the chapter. However, this process only works if it takes place within the boundaries of a clear and explicit strategic direction for the company—set down by top management.

Recommendations for innovation often proclaim that you need to "think outside of the box," and "get out of your comfort zone." However, what Burgelman observed, in studying the innovation processes of many high-tech companies, is that people need some sort of a box to channel their creativity, in the form of a clear strategic intent. This description of a company's general strategic direction should not be overly narrow, in which case it stifles creative new ideas. But people need a general direction to provide boundary conditions between which they can innovate.

Intel's explicit boundaries were that it wanted to be at the forefront of semiconductor technology, aimed at the memory business. Hence, ideas that were clearly out-side the realm of semiconductors would automatically be selected out—in fact, employees would not even propose them. Sadler's Wells had the intent "to be the centre of innovation in dance" (e.g., other art forms were out), whereas Fremantle aimed to make television produc-tions that were replicable in other countries, with spill-over into other media (e.g., country-specific programs are immediately rejected). The strategic intent provides a limited set of boundaries, leaving ample room for innovation. Without such boundaries, coherence is lost, and there is no common basis that could give the firm a competitive advantage. (See table 11-2.)

TABLE 11-2

Five design rules for a selection system

1. **Enable selection to happen.**	Resist the temptation to pick and choose yourself. Your responsibility is to design the system.
2. **Tap into the wisdom of your crowd.**	Use the knowledge of many employees. Do not rely on the opinions of individuals to select among proposals.
3. **Objectivize the process.**	Design decision rules before needing to make concrete choices. Quantify them if you can.
4. **Let the evidence match the investment.**	Do not insist on numbers (e.g., market projections, payback time) too early in the process. Systematically gather evidence that aids decisions later in the process.
5. **Give people a box for channeling creativity.**	Create clear boundaries that individuals can innovate between. Don't make them too narrow.

Strategy Follows Innovation

Selection happens at every company. But too few think about and organize selection deliberately and systematically, with a clear strategy in mind. They just let it happen. Sometimes this may work, but a more systematic approach, which I outlined earlier, should increase the odds of true innovation happening within a firm.

Most of the innovations emerging from such a system will be incremental yet nice additions to your portfolio. Some could be big and might end up generating a significant new revenue stream for your firm. One or two, however, might end up changing the entire strategic direction of your company.

FIGURE 11-1

Variation and selection

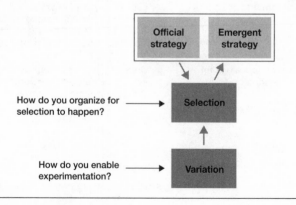

For example, the invention of the microprocessor changed the general strategic direction of the entire Intel Corporation—and with much success—away from memory into logic. At the British model-train-maker Hornby, the development of highly detailed scale models (rather than the more rudimentary toy trains) ended up shifting the company's strategy away from the toy market into the hobby and collectors' market—not something it had anticipated in advance. Who knows, Hornby's alliances with software and digital electronics companies might one day steer it somewhere else yet again. Innovation, in that sense, can provide for a bottom-up-driven process of strategy development.

Consider the simple model of variation and selection in figure 11-1. At the bottom are "variation" initiatives. The second step, above it, represents the firm's selection system, which will automatically terminate many of these ideas and initiatives while providing resources for the remaining ones. It's guided by the company's current strategy— providing "the box" that defines the rough boundaries for employees to innovate within. Yet, some of these initiatives might end up shifting the box, resulting in a new strategy.

This new strategy will not be a big jump away from the old one. It needs to build on at least part of the company's existing resources and capabilities, so it cannot be—and should not be—a leap into something entirely new. Intel's new focus on microprocessors, for example, still ensured that it stayed within the realm of semiconductors. Hornby still made model trains. But these were significant strategic shifts for these companies, away from outdated strategies and practices.

The purpose of a system of continual innovation is to make sure that a company does not get stuck using antiquated practices and strategies and, instead, automatically breaks away from them when they are no longer appropriate.

———————

Following these recommendations will make your firm varied yet selective. This will help reinvigorate a maturing business, sloughing off practices on a continual basis that are gradually growing old and antiquated.

Without such organizational measures in place, companies will eventually inevitably fall prey to bad habits and practices. Some become the topic of corporate biographies that document their rise but also their subsequent fall. The measures and recommendations described in this book should help you to better understand the outdated norms that populate your firm and others in your industry. It provides a guideline on how to rid your firm of bad habits. Mostly, I hope that it has inspired you to defy industry norms and turn your defiance into a source of innovation.

People sometimes ask me why I chose to become a professor in organization science—a professor of strategy and entrepreneurship, to be precise—instead of some other field like psychology, physics, or medicine. The superficial answer is that, for some reason, I was simply attracted to the study of organizations. But one can indeed wonder why. Why study organizations?

I think the deeper answer is that organizations are the fundamental building blocks of human life. Our ability to organize—into constellations of hundreds and even thousands of individuals, conducting tasks beyond any individual's comprehension—is arguably the one thing that sets us apart from other species (and other species of hominids for that matter). It has led us to dominate this planet—for better or for worse. We humans don't run particularly fast, are not very strong, nor are we exceptionally clever (Neanderthals had bigger brains than we do). But, gosh, are we good at getting organized.

Thousands of people can blend into an organization and develop patterns of interaction—processes, structures, and systems—that remain well after the original individuals have vanished. These organizations, in turn, interact with each other, exchanging knowledge, innovations, and ways of operating. Pretty much everything we touch, read, or otherwise consume has been produced by a constellation of organizations. Good things—innovations, practices, and ways of working—get passed on from one generation to the next in such an organization, and from one organization to the next one. That's how we make progress, and how our economies and societies take shape and prosper.

However, this implies that organizations have also taken on lives of their own. They have become entities in themselves. And this means that what is good for the organization is not necessarily always the best thing for the individuals that embody it, and vice versa. Similarly, the practices and ways of working have taken on lives of their own. And what is good for the spread and survival of these organizational traits is not always what is best for the company itself, let alone for the individuals who practice and populate them. Bad habits get passed on, and innovations that are harmful also spread through the network of interconnected firms.

But, as humans, we also possess the abilities of consciousness and volition, which we can use to identify and eliminate these practices. That's my take on innovation: no need to think of something novel and clever; just stop doing bad things (although, admittedly, that can be easier said than done).

I hope this book has given you some inspiration and guidelines to identify and eliminate your own bad practices and improve your organization to the benefit of all who rely on it.

NOTES

Introduction

1. Mihaela Stan and Freek Vermeulen, "Selection at the Gate: Difficult Cases, Spillovers, and Organizational Learning," *Organization Science* 24, no. 3 (May–June 2013): 796–812.

2. Natalie Mizik and Robert Jacobson, "Are Physicians 'Easy Marks'? Quantifying the Effects of Detailing and Sampling on New Prescriptions," *Management Science* 50, no. 12 (December 2004): 1704–1715.

Chapter 1

1. Sidney. G. Winter and Gabriel Szulanski, "Replication as Strategy," *Organization Science* 12 (2001): 730–743.

2. J. Richard Hackman and Ruth Wageman, "Total Quality Management: Empirical, Conceptual, and Practical Issues," *Administrative Science Quarterly* 40 (1995): 309–342.

3. Pamela R. Haunschild and Anne S. Miner, "Modes of Interorganizational Imitation: The Effects of Outcome Salience and Uncertainty," *Administrative Science Quarterly* 42 (1997): 472–500; Heather A. Haveman, "Follow the Leader: Mimetic Isomorphism and Entry into New Markets," *Administrative Science Quarterly* 38 (1993): 593–627.

4. Mark J. Zbaracki, "The Rhetoric and Reality of Total Quality Management," *Administrative Science Quarterly* 43 (1998): 602–636.

Chapter 2

1. Markus Reitzig and Stefan Wagner, "The Hidden Costs of Outsourcing: Evidence from Patent Data," *Strategic Management Journal* 31, no. 11 (2010): 1183–1201.

2. Mary J. Benner and Michael L. Tushman, "Process Management and Technological Innovation: A Longitudinal Study of the Photography and Paint Industries," *Administrative Science Quarterly* 47 (2002): 676–706; Mary J. Benner and Michael L. Tushman, "Exploitation, Exploration, and Process Management: The Productivity Dilemma Revisited," *Academy of Management Review* 28, no. 2 (2003): 238–256.

Chapter 3

1. See, for instance, William H. Durham, *Coevolution: Genes, Culture, and Human Diversity* (Palo Alto, CA: Stanford University Press, 1991).

Chapter 5

1. Liz Welch, "Entrepreneur Designs Upscale Hotels for Budget Travelers," *Inc.*, June 2014.

Chapter 6

1. Clayton M. Christensen, Dina Wang, and Derek van Bever "Consulting on the Cusp of Disruption," *Harvard Business Review*, October 2013.

2. "Enough Leadership. Time for Communityship," Henry Mintzberg blog, February 12, 2015, http://www.mintzberg.org/blog/communityship.

Chapter 7

1. Natalie Mizik and Robert Jacobson, "Are Physicians 'Easy Marks'? Quantifying the Effects of Detailing and Sampling on New Prescriptions," *Management Science* 50, no. 12 (December 2004): 1704–1715.

2. Solomon E. Asch, "Studies of Independence and Conformity: I. A Minority of One Against a Unanimous Majority," *Psychological Monographs: General and Applied* 70, no. 9 (1956): 1–70; and Wendy Wood et al., "Minority Influence: A Meta-Analytic Review of Social Influence Processes," *Psychological Bulletin* 115, no. 3 (May 1994): 323–345.

Chapter 8

1. For example, Ranjay Gulati and Pahish Puranam, "Renewal Through Reorganizations: The Value of Inconsistencies Between Formal and Informal Organization," *Organization Science* 20, no. 2 (2009): 422–440.

2. See, for instance, Daniel A. Levinthal and James G. March, "The Myopia of Learning," *Strategic Management Journal* 14 (1993): 95–112; and Danny Miller, "The Architecture of Simplicity," *Academy of Management Review* 18, no. 1 (January 1993): 116–138.

3. Alfred P. West, Jr., and Yoram (Jerry) Wind, "Putting the Organization on Wheels: Workplace Design at SEI," *California Management Review* 49, no. 2 (Winter 2007): 138–153.

4. For example, Jeffrey Pfeffer and Gerald R. Salancik, "Organizational Decision Making as a Political Process: The Case of a University Budget," *Administrative Science Quarterly* 19, no. 2 (June 1973): 135–151.

5. Nitin Nohria, "Appex Corp." Harvard Business School Case 491-082, February 1991 (Revised February 1992).

Chapter 9

1. Mihaela Stan and Freek Vermeulen, "Selection at the Gate: Difficult Cases, Spillovers, and Organizational Learning," *Organization Science* 24, no. 3 (May–June 2013): 796–812.

2. Cristina Gibson and Freek Vermeulen, "A Healthy Divide: Subgroups as a Stimulus for Team Learning Behavior," *Administrative Science Quarterly* 48, no. 2 (June 2003): 202–239.

Chapter 10

1. James G. March, "Exploration and Exploitation in Organizational Learning," *Organization Science* 2, no. 1 (March 1991): 71–87.

2. Jack A. Nickerson and Todd R. Zenger, "Being Efficiently Fickle: A Dynamic Theory of Organizational Choice," *Organization Science* 13, no. 5 (September–October 2002): 547–566; and Ranjay Gulati and Phanish Puranam, "Renewal Through Reorganization: The Value of Inconsistencies Between Formal and Informal Organization," *Organization Science* 20, no. 2 (March–April 2009): 422–440.

Chapter 11

1. See Lukas F. Keller and Donald M. Waller, "Inbreeding Effects in Wild Populations," *Trends in Ecology & Evolution* 17, no. 5 (May 2002): 230–241; Pär K. Ingvarsson, "Restoration of Genetic Variation Lost—The Genetic Rescue Hypothesis," *Trends in Ecology & Evolution* 16, no. 2 (February 2001): 62–63.

2. Freek Vermeulen, "How Acquisitions Can Revitalize Companies," *MIT Sloan Management Review* 46, no. 4 (Summer 2005): 45–51.

3. Robert A. Burgelman, "Fading Memories: A Process Theory of Strategic Business Exit in Dynamic Environment," *Administrative Science Quarterly* 39, no. 1 (March 1994): 24–56.

4. Robert A. Burgelman, *Strategy is Destiny: How Strategy-Making Shapes a Company's Future* (New York: Free Press, 2002).

5. See, for instance, Barry M. Staw, "The Escalation of Commitment To a Course of Action," *Academy of Management Review* 16, no. 4 (October 1981): 577–587; Kai-Yu Hsieh, Wenpin Tsai and Ming-Jer Chen, "If They Can Do It, Why Not Us? Competitors as Reference Points for Justifying Escalation of Commitment," *Academy of Management Journal* 58, no. 1 (February 2015): 38–58; and Timo O. Vuori and Quy N. Huy, "Distributed Attention and Shared Emotions in the Innovation Process: How Nokia Lost the Smartphone Battle," *Administrative Science Quarterly* 61, no. 1 (2016): 9–51.

6. Burgelman, *Strategy is Destiny*.

INDEX

acquisitions, 212–215
airline industry, 100–101,
　114–115, 117, 118
association with success. *See*
　success and association
　with success

bad habits. *See* bad practices
bad practices
　acceptance of status quo,
　　64, 65, 66
　causal ambiguity's role in (*see*
　　causal ambiguity)
　counterproductiveness of
　　some best practices, 9
　discovering why newspapers
　　are so large, 63–66
　ease of spread of (*see*
　　persistence of bad
　　practices)
　experimenting with change,
　　67–68
　lure of association with
　　success (*see* success and
　　association with success)

potential in eliminating,
　17–18, 68–69
reasons that organizations
　employ, 10–12
spread of within industries, 10
ten commandments for
　breaking (*see* identifying
　and eliminating bad
　practices)
value of best practices, 8–9
Beacon Press, 39
benchmarking
　cutting out the practice,
　　98–99
　reverse, 99–101
　replication of success and,
　　29–31
Benner, Mary, 47–51, 205
best practices. *See* bad practices
British Telecom (BT), 188, 211
Brown, Shona, 192
bundles of practices, 113–116
Burgelman, Robert, 219, 225
business models, 113–116
buyback guarantees, 38–39,
　69, 109

ABOUT THE AUTHOR

Freek Vermeulen is a professor of strategy and entrepreneurship at the London Business School. He is the first-ever winner of the school's Excellence in Teaching Award and has received various international prizes for his research on strategic management, and particularly for his application of rigorous research to improve the practice of management. Freek writes regularly for *Harvard Business Review*, the *Financial Times*, *Forbes*, and the *Wall Street Journal*, among others. In the past, the *Financial Times* described him as a "rising star" and a "new management guru."